How to play

Bridge

Jeremy Flint

Illustrated by Hana Feuerstein

Hamlyn

London · New York · Sydney · Toronto

Contents

Published by.
The Hamlyn Publishing Group Limited
London · New York · Sydney · Toronto
Astronaut House, Feltham, Middlesex, England

© Copyright The Hamlyn Publishing Group Limited 1977
Third Impression 1981

ISBN 0 600 31397 2

Printed in Italy

Introduction

The aim of this book is to explain how to
play Contract Bridge. No prior knowledge
of any sort is required. All you need is a
pack of cards and a little perseverance.
 There are two main parts of Bridge—
the bidding and the card play. I have
concentrated rather more on the bidding.
There are techniques in card play that can
be taught, such as the establishment of
tricks and the choosing of the best lead,
and these techniques I have outlined, but
generally speaking skill in play comes
automatically with experience.
 The basic ideas of bidding, on the other
hand, have to be taught.
 The bidding methods described are
those of Natural systems, the most widely
used methods in Great Britain and the
USA.

Chapter One

An Outline

Contract Bridge is a card game for four players. It has the reputation of being a difficult game. That is not the case. But it is an *extensive* game; by that I mean that it has several different aspects, all of which a player has to master to become competent. To take an example, no one aspect of Bridge is more difficult than Poker; but there are at least half a dozen aspects of Bridge of equivalent complexity to Poker, and so correspondingly it does take longer to learn to play Bridge.

Bridge is played with an ordinary pack or deck of 52 playing cards. For the benefit of anyone who has led an unusually sheltered life, there are four different suits in a pack of cards: spades, hearts, diamonds and clubs. Each suit has thirteen cards. For the purposes of bridge the thirteen cards are ranked as follows, starting at the bottom: two, three, four, five, six, seven, eight, nine, ten, jack, queen, king, ace.

A Hand of Rubber Bridge

Rather than go through the rules of each part of the game step by step, I am going to start by describing the play of a complete hand of bridge. The purpose of this description is to show you the general form that the game takes. When you have got that fixed in your mind, the detailed descriptions of the individual parts will have more meaning. Most of the detail will seem bewildering; but then if you were watching a tennis match for the first time that would also be confusing. But at the end of the set you would at least have a general idea of the form of the game. That is the object of this first chapter.

The hand I am going to describe is the first hand of a *rubber* of bridge. There are two variations of bridge, *rubber* and *duplicate*. In most respects they are identical, but where there are any differences this book describes the practice at rubber bridge.

A rubber has the following parts:

1. The cut for deal and partnerships

2. Several deals: each deal has the following phases:
a) the auction
b) the play
c) the scoring.
3. Final score and settlement.

Partnerships. The four players play in two partnerships. At the beginning of a rubber the partnerships are determined by each player drawing a card from the pack. The two players with the highest cards play together against the two drawing the lowest cards. If two players draw a card of the same *rank* (e.g. two players both draw queens) then the higher card is the one whose suit ranks higher: in bridge the lowest ranking suit is clubs, followed in order by diamonds, hearts and spades. Let us assume that the players draw the following cards: ten of clubs, four of hearts, ten of diamonds and queen of hearts. Then the players drawing the queen of hearts and ten of diamonds play together against the other two.

The player who draws the highest card has the choice of seat, and he is also the first *dealer*. It is usual to label the four positions at the table North, South, East and West, as shown below.

Let us assume that the player drawing the queen of diamonds chooses to sit in the North seat. Then his partner sits opposite, in the South seat, and the opponents take up the East-West seats.

Dealing the Cards. It is convenient though not absolutely essential to have two packs of cards, with different coloured backs. The cards are shuffled by the player on the dealer's left. Say North chooses to deal the blue cards. Then East shuffles the blues, and when he has finished he places them on his right. North then picks them up and passes them over to West, who cuts the pack into two portions. North picks up the original bottom portion of the pack, places it on top of the original top portion, and commences to deal the cards. He gives the first card to the player immediately on his left and continues distributing them one at a time in a clockwise direction until the whole pack is dealt and everyone has 13 cards. While he is doing this South is shuffling the other pack of cards, and when he has finished he puts the pack on his right, between himself and East.

You may think this ritual is rather ponderous and unnecessary. But in practice it is quite important, first of all to ensure that the cards are properly shuffled after every deal, and secondly to keep track of whose turn it is to deal. The dealer of the next hand is the player immediately to the current dealer's left, East in this case. This is indicated by the fact that the second pack of cards is currently on his left.

When all the cards have been dealt each each player picks up his cards and arranges them into suits, holding them such that the other players cannot see them.

In this first deal of the rubber, the cards fall as shown in Figure 1.

Fig. 1

♠ 8 6 3 2
♥ J 10 5 4
♦ 4
♣ A 8 3 2

♠ A Q 4
♥ 9 8 7
♦ 10 9 2
♣ J 9 7 6

N
W E
S

♠ 5
♥ A K 3
♦ A Q J 8 7 5
♣ Q 5 4

♠ K J 10 9 7
♥ Q 6 2
♦ K 6 3
♣ K 10

The auction

After the players have picked up their cards and sorted them, the *auction* starts. The auction is the process by which the final *contract* is determined. The players take it in turns to make *calls*, with the dealer making the first call.

In this case North is the dealer and he *passes*. That is to say, for the moment he does not want to make a bid, though that does not prohibit him from re-entering the auction at a later stage. In the UK players often indicate a pass by saying 'No bid' or

'No'; in the USA players usually say 'Pass'.

After North passes, it becomes East's turn to make a call. He bids *One Diamond*. A *bid* is an undertaking for the partnership to take six tricks *plus* the number named in the bid, with the suit that is named as trumps. The next chapter explains the details of trick-taking. So in this case East's One Diamond bid is an undertaking by his side to take seven tricks with diamonds as trumps.

After a player has made a bid, any subsequent bid must outrank the previous bid, just as in any other type of auction. The rules of this are as follows:
a) any bid at a higher level outranks the previous bid;
b) among bids at the same level, the order of precedence is Clubs (lowest), then Diamonds, Hearts, Spades, and finally No-Trumps. At No-Trumps there is no trump suit.

It is now South's turn to call, and he bids *One Spade*. In other words, he says that his side will take seven tricks with spades as trumps. He does not have to raise the level, as spades outrank diamonds.

West in his turn bids *One No-Trump*. Again he does not have to raise the level, as no-trumps outrank spades.

North now comes back into the auction. You will remember that he passed as dealer but now he bids *Two Spades*. Notice that he had to go to the two level to out-bid West's One No-Trump.

Over Two Spades East bids *Three No-Trumps*. Two No-Trumps would be sufficient to outbid North's Two Spades, but when you come to the chapter on scoring you will see that there is an advantage to be gained by bidding to Three No-Trumps.

South has nothing further to add, so he passes, and so do West and North. The three successive passes end the auction. (The only time when there can be a call after three passes is on the first round of the auction). The *final contract* is thus *Three No-Trumps*, and so East-West will be attempting to make nine tricks at No-Trumps.

In future this complete auction will be written as follows:

South	*West*	*North*	*East*
–	–	Pass	1♦
1♠	1NT	2♠	3NT
Pass	Pass	Pass	

9

The Play. After the auction is over the *play* commences. The first player of the partnership to mention the denomination of the final contract is called the **declarer**, and his partner is the **dummy**. The other two players are the **defenders**. In this case the final denomination is No-Trumps, and West was the first player of the East-West partnership to mention No-Trumps, so he becomes the declarer and East is dummy.

The play of the hand is started by the player immediately to the declarer's left. He has to make the **opening lead**. This means he takes a card from his hand and places it face up on the table. In our example he leads the two of spades.

After the opening lead the dummy spreads his hand on the table with the cards arranged in suits. If it is a trump contract he should put the trump suit on his right, but in No-Trump contracts there is no preferred order. After dummy has put down his hand he takes no further part in the play, apart from having one or two minor rights in trying to prevent his partner from making illegal plays.

When the dummy has been exposed the declarer will usually take a minute or two to weigh up the situation. He is in charge of the play for both his own hand and the dummy, while each defender (in this case North and South) only has his own thirteen cards to play.

The declarer eventually plays the five of spades from dummy, and now South has to play. He puts on the king of spades, and now West *wins* the trick with the ace of spades. A trick is a collection of four cards, and the play consists of the contest for the thirteen tricks available on any deal.

At trick two, West as the winner of the previous trick leads the ten of diamonds from his hand. North plays the four of diamonds, the declarer plays the five from dummy, and South plays the three of diamonds, allowing the ten to win.

As West has won the trick it is still him to play at the third trick. He leads the two

of diamonds, North plays the three of spades, West plays the jack of diamonds from dummy and now South wins with the king of diamonds.

South now has to lead to the fourth trick. He leads the jack of spades. West plays the queen of spades, North the six of spades and East the four of clubs. This leaves the position in Figure 2, each player now having played four cards:

Fig. 2

The interest of the deal is now over, and in practice West would lay down his hand saying 'I claim six more tricks: the ace and king of hearts, and four diamond tricks.' This makes nine tricks in all so West has fulfilled his contract of Three No-Trumps.

Now comes the *scoring*, described in detail in Chapter Three. For the moment, we will just note that for making their Three No-Trump contract East-West score a **game**. The rubber is over when one side has scored two games, so there are always at least two hands in a rubber, though there are often many more.

You may have found this all rather confusing. But if you have read it with the attitude I suggested, at least you will have some idea of the general framework. In the next three chapters I will discuss in more detail the basic rules of trick-taking, scoring and bidding.

Chapter Two

Tricks and Trick-taking

The whole game of Bridge revolves round trick-taking. The bidding consists of offers to take certain numbers of tricks; the play is concerned with the conflict between the two sides in trying either to fulfil or to defeat that offer.

A *trick* is a collection of four cards, one from each player. The player **on lead** plays the first card to the trick. Except for the opening lead, the player on lead is the player who won the previous trick. In the case of the **opening lead**, the first lead in the play of the hand, the leader is the defender on the declarer's left. In either case, the players play to the trick in clockwise order round the table.

There is one simple rule about playing to a trick; if a player has cards of the suit led he must play one of those cards. This is referred to as **following suit**. If he has no cards in the suit led (referred to as being **void**) he can play any other card he likes. The leader to the trick is allowed to lead any card he likes.

The **winner** of the trick is determined as follows:
a) if the trick contains no cards of the trump suit, then the card that wins the trick is the highest card in the suit led.
b) if the trick contains cards from the trump suit, the card that wins the trick is the highest trump in the trick. Clearly in a No-Trump contract rule (b) never comes into effect.

Examples
In each of the examples below the card led is the first named. Diamonds are trumps.
a) ♥2 ♥3 ♥K ♥A. The ace of hearts is the highest heart in the trick, and so wins the trick.
b) ♥Q ♥6 ♥7 ♣2. The queen of hearts wins the trick.
c) ♣2 ♥Q ♥6 ♥7. Now the two of clubs wins the trick, as it was led and it is the only club in the trick. Notice the difference the lead makes – the cards in the tricks in (b) and (c) are exactly the same.

d) ♠Q ♠K ♠A ♦2. The two of diamonds wins the trick as it is the only trump in the trick. Note that the smallest trump beats the highest card in any other suit.
e) ♠Q ♠K ♦5 ♦6. Now the six of diamonds wins the trick, it being the highest trump in the trick.

Since the players play as a partnership it doesn't matter which of them wins the trick from the point of view of the final tally. Many of the tactics of the play are to do with the co-operation between the partners to win tricks.

Trick Establishment
The methods of setting up tricks can be seen most clearly from the declarer's point of view. Remember he is the player who is in charge of the dummy, so he can determine both the cards played by his side to a trick. The defence has a more difficult task, although the principles are the same.

Trumps produce a complicating element, so the first part of this chapter considers the play within one suit when there are no trumps.

To start off, Figure 3 is a combination you cannot get wrong.

Fig. 3 *Declarer* A K Q | W E | *Dummy* 6 5 4

No matter how he plays this suit, the declarer must make three tricks. But now make the lay-out as in Figure 4 and one

Fig. 4 A K 6 | W E | Q 5 4

occasionally sees beginners going wrong. To make three tricks obviously the declarer must avoid playing two of the high cards on the same trick. Otherwise there is nothing to it. The importance of suits like the above is that they give the declarer

11

flexibility, to enable him to place the lead to the next trick in either hand.

Fig. 5 K Q J | W E | 8 7 6

In Figure 5 the defence holds the ace, and the declarer can only take two tricks in the suit. To take the two tricks the declarer must lead the suit to force out the defence's *stopper* (so called because it *stops* the run of the suit).

Let's see how these notions work in practice. In the deal below West is the declarer in a contract of Three No-Trumps. As you will remember, that means he has to make nine tricks. North leads the jack of spades.

Fig. 6

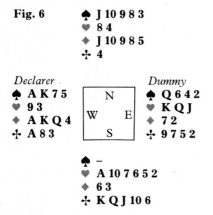

♠ J 10 9 8 3
♥ 8 4
♦ J 10 9 8 5
♣ 4

Declarer
♠ A K 7 5
♥ 9 3
♦ A K Q 4
♣ A 8 3

Dummy
♠ Q 6 4 2
♥ K Q J
♦ 7 2
♣ 9 7 5 2

♠ –
♥ A 10 7 6 5 2
♦ 6 3
♣ K Q J 10 6

When you are declarer it is most important to get into the habit of making a *plan*. In this instance the first thing you should do, before playing from dummy, is to count your certain winners. In Figure 6 you have three in spades (the ace, king and queen), three in diamonds (again the ace, king and queen) and one in clubs. That makes seven, and so you need two more from somewhere. On this hand it is easy enough to spot where these are coming from. The heart combination will produce two tricks once you have knocked out the ace. But there are still one or two pitfalls. Having made your plan you might win the spade in hand and play off some of your top winners. If those winners included the ace of clubs, when you eventually played a heart South would be able to win with the ace and cash four club tricks. So the defence would have taken five tricks before you had taken your nine. It is easy to avoid this type of trap if you remember to *play*

on the suits where you have top losers first.

The other way you can go wrong on this hand is by being sloppy with **entries**. An entry is a high card which enables you to place the lead for the next trick. See what happens if you foolishly play the queen of spades on the first trick. Following the precept I outline above, you lead the king of hearts at trick two. But South is not obliged to take his ace immediately, and if he is wise he will **hold up** for one round. When you play another heart he will take his ace and play a high club, and you will find yourself stranded in your hand. Your ninth trick for your three no-trump contract will be sitting in dummy, but you will have no way of getting at it.

Of course what you should do is win the first spade in your hand (i.e. the West hand). Now when you play hearts it will not avail South to hold up his ace, because you will be able to enter dummy with the queen of spades to cash the third heart.

Finally notice that if North had led a club there was no way you could have made the contract–South would have continued clubs until you took your ace, and so he would have made five tricks before you had your nine. This is a good example of the importance of the opening lead.

A number of intresting points are illustrated by this hand. Go over it several times until you are sure you have grasped them.

Trick establishment is not confined to positions where the defence has only the ace. In the holding in Figure 7 West can

Fig. 7 Q J 9 8 4 | W E | 10 7 3

establish three tricks by knocking out the ace and king; and with Figure 8 he can

Fig. 8 J 10 9 8 | W E | 7 6 4

establish one trick by leading the suit three times, to knock out the ace, king and queen.

Long-card Tricks

In the previous section I discussed methods of establishing tricks by driving out the opponents' aces and kings. Sometimes their stoppers have a different form. Look at Figures 9 and 10.

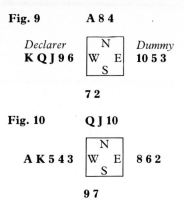

Fig. 9 A 8 4

Declarer K Q J 9 6   Dummy 10 5 3

7 2

Fig. 10 Q J 10

A K 5 4 3   8 6 2

9 7

In Figure 9 we have the type of holding I have already discussed: after North has taken his ace the declarer makes four tricks in the suit.

In Figure 10 the defence do not have the ace or king. But just as surely they prevent the run of the suit. However the declarer can establish four tricks for himself by losing the lead once to North. In general he will do that on the first or second round of the suit. It makes no difference within the suit if he plays ace, king and a small one; or ace then small, or small immediately; but by keeping back a high honour he gives himself an extra *entry*. That can be the difference between making a slam and going down.

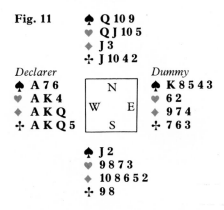

Fig. 11 ♠ Q 10 9
♥ Q J 10 5
♦ J 3
♣ J 10 4 2

Declarer
♠ A 7 6
♥ A K 4
♦ A K Q
♣ A K Q 5

Dummy
♠ K 8 5 4 3
♥ 6 2
♦ 9 7 4
♣ 7 6 3

♠ J 2
♥ 9 8 7 3
♦ 10 8 6 5 2
♣ 9 8

In Figure 11 you are the declarer as West, but this time the contract is Six No-Trumps. (When you come to the chapter on scoring you will find that there is an extra advantage in bidding a six or seven contract). North leads the queen of hearts.

As in the previous hand, you don't play a card from dummy until you have made a plan of campaign. On this hand you can count ten top tricks: two in spades, two in hearts, three in diamonds and three in

clubs. So you need two more from somewhere. The only place they can come from is the spade suit. You note that provided the outstanding five spades break three and two, then after losing one spade trick dummy's lowly four and three will be tricks.

Having decided that, the average beginner then splashes out ace and king of spades and another spade. The four and three are now tricks, but there is no way to get at them. Of course the solution is to play ace of spades and then a low spade playing *low* (or **ducking**) from dummy. Thus North wins his spade trick on the *second* round of the suit, and now when West subsequently leads his third spade to dummy's king, he is in dummy to cash the winners.

Notice that there was a potential long-card trick in the West hand. If the outstanding clubs had been divided three and three, they would all fall on the ace, king and queen and West's five would have been a fourth round winner. However that did not enter the calculations on this hand, as it would only provide *one* extra trick, and *two* were required. On this hand it would have been wrong to have played off three top clubs before playing spades, as now when North won the second spade he would have been able to cash a club.

You will find these two twin themes occur time and again when you are playing the dummy: first of all you must find a way of making the number of tricks you require, and secondly you must prevent the defence from making the number that they require.

Other types of holding for which you can develop long-card tricks are given in Figures 12 and 13.

Fig. 12 Q J 9

A 5 4   K 7 3 2

10 8 6

In Figure 12 after one trick has been lost East's fourth card will score.

Fig. 13 9 7

8 3 2   K Q 6 5 4

A J 10

13

Figure 13 illustrates a combination of techniques: a trick must be lost to a top card, the ace, and to a long card. So South takes two tricks, but eventually the East holding is worth three tricks.

The Finesse

So far it has not mattered which of the defenders holds the stoppers. But look at the combinations in Figures 14 and 15.

Fig. 14   K 3

```
        N
6 5   W   E   A Q
        S
```

        8 4

Fig. 15   8 3

```
        N
6 5   W   E   A Q
        S
```

        K 4

In Figure 14 East-West can make two tricks in the suit if West leads towards the ace-queen and covers whichever card North plays. In Figure 15, when East plays the queen on North's three South will win the king. The ace-queen holding is worth one trick or two according to which defender holds the king. That is the essence of the *finesse*. The ace-queen combination is called a *tenace*.

Notice that the lead has to come up to the tenace holding in order for it to be worth an extra trick. If West were on lead from his ace-queen holding he could only make one trick. And if South had to lead in Figure 15 he would not make his king.

All of the following lay-outs have this same notion of finesse, and in all of them it is necessary for the lead to come up to the tenace.

Fig. 16   K 5 4

```
          N
Q J 10   W   E   A 8 3
          S
```

        7 6 2

In Figure 16 West must lead the queen to trap North's king.

Fig. 17   Q 7 2

```
        N
A 8 4   W   E   K J 3
        S
```

        10 6 5

In Figure 17 West leads towards the king-jack.

Fig. 18   Q 7 3

```
          N
A 10 4   W   E   K J 9
          S
```

        (Q 6 5)

The two queens in Figure 18 are not misprints. This situation illustrates a *two-way* finesse. If the declarer decides to place North with the queen, he plays ace and another; if South has the queen, then the winning play is small to the king and small back to the ten.

Fig. 19   A 8 2

```
        N
9 7 6   W   E   K Q 5 3
        S
```

        J 10 4

To restrict the defence to one trick in Figure 19 the declarer must lead twice toward the king-queen holding.

Fig. 20   A K J 3

```
        N
9 7 4   W   E   Q 8 2
        S
```

        10 6 5

Figure 20 is not a promising holding for East-West to make a trick, but the best chance is to find North with both the ace and king. Again West has to lead twice towards the queen.

Trumps

We have already seen the process by which a trump wins a trick – the trick is won by the highest trump, no matter what the make-up of the non-trump (or *plain* or *side-suit*) cards played. The side that wins the contract in a particular suit clearly expects to do better by having that suit as trumps, than say, if they had played in no-trumps.

There are several ways in which the power of trumps can be exploited.

Ruffing Losers

Fig. 21

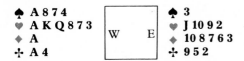

♠ A 8 7 4   ♠ 3
♥ A K Q 8 7 3   ♥ J 10 9 2
♦ A   ♦ 10 8 7 6 3
♣ A 4   ♣ 9 5 2

In Figure 21, West's three little spades are *losers*. That is, if he doesn't find some way of getting rid of them he will eventually lose three spade tricks. But if East-West are playing in a heart contract, West can trump (or **ruff**) his losing spades with East's trumps. Say the lead is a diamond: West wins with the ace, plays ace of spades and another spade putting on the nine of hearts, returns a club to his ace, ruffs another spade with the ten of hearts, plays the two of hearts to his ace, ruffs a spade with the jack of hearts, and finally ruffs a diamond with a high trump and plays out his top trumps. All he loses is the four of clubs.

But notice that West could only afford one round of trumps. If he had played two rounds before he had ruffed his three losing spades he would have been left with a losing spade at the end.

Stopping the Opponents' Long Suit

Fig. 22

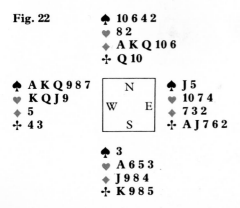

         ♠ 10 6 4 2
         ♥ 8 2
         ♦ A K Q 10 6
         ♣ Q 10

♠ A K Q 9 8 7   ♠ J 5
♥ K Q J 9   ♥ 10 7 4
♦ 5   ♦ 7 3 2
♣ 4 3   ♣ A J 7 6 2

         ♠ 3
         ♥ A 6 5 3
         ♦ J 9 8 4
         ♣ K 9 8 5

East-West in Figure 22 are in Four Spades. North leads the king then the ace of diamonds. West ruffs the second round. Now East's trumps are no use to him, so he

plays a trump to the jack, then one back to his ace. He notes that South discards a diamond on the second round, marking North with four trumps. So West continues with the king and queen, pulling North's remaining trumps and leaving himself with a small one. Now West plays hearts, and when South eventually takes his ace West has still got a trump to prevent North-South from taking tricks in diamonds.

Establishing a Side-suit

Fig. 23

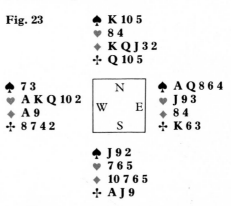

         ♠ K 10 5
         ♥ 8 4
         ♦ K Q J 3 2
         ♣ Q 10 5

♠ 7 3   ♠ A Q 8 6 4
♥ A K Q 10 2   ♥ J 9 3
♦ A 9   ♦ 8 4
♣ 8 7 4 2   ♣ K 6 3

         ♠ J 9 2
         ♥ 7 6 5
         ♦ 10 7 6 5
         ♣ A J 9

In Figure 23 West plays in Four Hearts and North leads the king of diamonds. As he does not relish a switch to clubs West wins with the ace and leads a low spade to the queen. That wins, so he continues with ace of spades and a spade ruffed with the ace of trumps. North and South have each followed three times to the spades, so dummy's two remaining spades are winners. So now all that remains is to play king of hearts and a heart to the nine. When all follow the last of the defence's trumps is removed with dummy's jack, West being careful to play the ten. Now dummy's two spade tricks are taken.

Chapter Three

Scoring

The object of Bridge is to score as many points as possible There are two types of points:
a) the trick score
b) bonus points.

The importance of the division is that the first variety can accumulate to produce **games**. The side that first wins two games wins the **rubber**, and with it a bonus. So the first variety of points can eventually produce points in addition to their value as written down on the score card.

The Scoring Pad

It is usual in rubber bridge to score on a pad like the one shown in Figure 24.

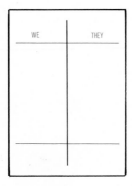

Fig. 24

Naturally enough points scored by your side go in the 'We' column, and points scored by the opponents go in the 'They' column. The line going across the pad about two thirds of the way down is used to separate the two classes of points. Points for trick-score go below the line, and points for bonuses go above the line.

Trick Score

The trick score is awarded for the number of tricks *contracted for* in a successful contract. The amount per trick varies with the denomination.

Clubs Diamonds	20 points
Hearts Spades	30 points
No-Trumps	40 points for first trick 30 points for subsequent tricks.

Some examples may make this clearer. If you take nine tricks in a contract of Three Hearts you get 90 points below the line. If you made ten tricks you would still only get 90 below, but you would get a bonus of 30 points above the line for the extra trick. If however you made ten tricks and had bid Four Hearts you would get 120 points below the line.

Game. You score a game when you get 100 points below the line. You can do it in steps, or you can do it on one hand by bidding a **game contract**. Clearly then a game contract is one with a trick score of 100 points or more. Thus you need to bid and make Five Clubs or Five Diamonds to score a game, Four Hearts or Four Spades, or Three No-Trumps. Much of the bidding is concerned with the decision of whether or not to try for a game.

Any contract which scores less than a game is called a **part-score**. Part-scores may be added together to produce a game. But as soon as one side gets a game a line is drawn across the score pad, and now both sides have to start from scratch to score the next game.

Vulnerability. A side which has scored a game is described as being **vulnerable**. The effect of this is to increase the stakes: the penalties for failing to make contracts are higher, and some of the bonuses for success are higher.

Bonuses and Penalties

Winning the Rubber

The side that first gets two games wins the rubber, and if the opponents have not scored a game the winning side gets 700 points; if the opponents have scored a game the winners get 500 points.

If a rubber is abandoned unfinished, a side which is a game ahead gets 300 points, a side with a live part-score gets 50 points.

Overtricks
Tricks scored in excess of the contract bring a bonus above the line at the rate per trick described in the previous section. That is, overtricks in a minor suit contract score 20 a trick, in a major suit or no-trumps 30 per trick.

Slam Contracts
A *Small Slam* is a contract of Six in some denomination. A *Grand Slam* is a contract at the Seven level. Since the trick score is more than 100 points, success in these contracts scores a game. But there are additional bonuses:
a) Small Slam
Not vulnerable, 500 points
Vulnerable,   750 points
b) Grand Slam
Not vulnerable, 1000 points
Vulnerable,   1500 points

Undertricks
If one side fails to make its contract it has to pay a penalty above the line to the other side for each trick by which it fails. Not vulnerable, each undertrick gives 50 points to the other side; vulnerable each undertrick cost 100 points.

Honours
If any individual player holds four of the top five trump honours (i.e. any four out of ace, king, queen, jack, ten) his side gets a bonus of 100 points. If he holds five his side gets 150 points. At no-trumps, a bonus of 150 points is obtained for a player holding all four aces.

Doubles and Redoubles
If a defender does not think the declaring side is going to make its contract he can *double*. As with other calls, a player may only double when it is his turn to bid, and he may only double a contract bid by the other side.

After a contract has been doubled, the declaring side may *redouble*.

The general effect of doubles and redoubles is to increase the penalties for failing to make the contract, but also to increase the score for fulfilling the contract.

Undertricks
The first doubled undertrick not vulnerable gives 100 points to the defending side. Subsequent undertricks give 200 points each. Vulnerable, the first trick costs 200 points, and each subsequent trick costs 300.

If the contract is redoubled all the above penalties are multiplied by two.

Successful Contracts
In doubled contracts the trick score is doubled. So if the declaring side make eight tricks in two spades doubled they get 120 points below the line. In addition, there are extra bonuses for making over-tricks. Each non-vulnerable overtrick scores 100 points. Each vulnerable overtrick scores 200 points. And as before, redoubling multiplies all these scores by two. Finally there is an extra bonus of 50 points for making a doubled contract.

An Example Rubber
To illustrate these points I give below the score card of a typical rubber.
Hand 1. EW bid one No-Trump and make nine tricks. They score 40 below the line, and 60 above for the two over-tricks.
Hand 2. EW buy the contract in Three Hearts redoubled and make seven tricks. The two undertricks cost them 600 and are put onto the NS score (the first undertrick costs 200, the next one 400).
Hand 3. NS bid and make Six Hearts. North holds the five top hearts. They get 180 below the line, 500 above for the slam and 150 above for holding honours. Also a line is drawn across the pad to signify that a game has been scored.
Hand 4. EW make Three Clubs doubled with an overtrick. They get 120 below the line for the trick score, 100 above for the overtrick and 50 above for making a doubled contract. (Often the 50 is referred to as '50 for the insult'). They have scored a game so another line is drawn across the pad.
Hand 5. NS bid Six diamonds and make thirteen tricks. They score 120 below the line for the trick score, 20 above for the overtrick and 750 for the vulnerable slam. Since they have now obtained two games they have also won the rubber and as the opponents have a game NS get a bonus of 500.

The complete score card from the NS angle is shown in Figure 25. The numbers in square brackets refer to the hand on which the score was made.

17

WE	THEY
(+ 2450 NET)	
2820	370
500 [5]	
750 [5]	
20 [5]	
150 [3]	50 [4]
500 [3]	100 [4]
600 [2]	60 [1]
180 [3]	40 [1]
	120 [4]
120 [5]	

Fig. 25

Finally the points for each side are added up and the difference taken. NS have scored 2820 and EW 370, so NS have won the rubber by 2450 points. This is quite a big rubber; the average is around 1000 points.

When playing for stakes it is usual in the UK to play for so much a hundred, and to round odd 50s down. So at 10p a hundred NS would win £2·40 each. In the USA the stakes are usually expressed per point. At $\frac{1}{10}$ of a cent per point NS would win $2.45 each.

Chapter Four

The Language of Bidding

The Auction

The auction is the process by which the final contract is determined. Contested auctions, that is those in which all the players bid, are more complicated than those in which just one of the partnerships is involved, so at first I will just consider uncontested auctions.

Clearly if your partner were to put his hand face up on the table when it was his turn to bid you could decide what was the best contract. Or conversely, if you were to do that when it was your turn he could make the decision. Of course that is against the rules. But it does illustrate what the partners are trying to do in the bidding— each describes his hand in more and more detail with each successive bid, until one or other is in a position to announce the final contract.

There are two aspects to the decision:
a) in what denomination the final contract should be played
b) at what level.

As I discuss the details of the individual bids in the auction you will see how these considerations are dealt with.

Valuation

When you pick up your hand it is easy enough to see which is your longest suit, provided you are wearing your correct spectacles. But it is less obvious how *strong* your hand is. The final test of strength is how many tricks you and your partner can take between you. But at any rate in the early stages of the auction less direct methods of assessment are used.

An *average* hand is one with an average share of high cards. Since there are four aces, four kings, four queens and four jacks in the pack, Figure 26 is exactly average.

Fig. 26

It was easy enough to value this hand, as you had one of each of the high honours (not to mention one of each of the small or 'spot' cards as well). But make the hand as in Figure 27 and it is still about average, but not so immediately recognisable as such, since now we have replaced one ace by two queens. What we need is some quick way of expressing the fact that two queens are about equal to one ace. Much the most widely used method of doing this is the

Fig. 27

Fig. 30

Point Count.

High-card Points (HCP)

The honour cards are given the following values:

Ace   = 4
King   = 3
Queen = 2
Jack   = 1

So there are 40 points in the pack in honour cards, and an average hand will have a quarter of them, i.e. 10 points.

Notice that this scale assumes that, say, a king and a jack are equivalent to two queens, or that a king is equivalent to a queen and a jack. That has been the experience of good players over the years. The main fault of the scale is that it slightly undervalues aces.

This then is the first phase of our assessment of a hand. We add up the strength in terms of its high-card points (HCP).

Fig. 28

Fig. 29

The hand in Figure 28 has 16 HCP–1 in spades, 5 in hearts, 6 in diamonds, 4 in clubs, and is about an ace and a queen above average. The hand in Figure 29 has 3 HCP and is considerably below average. The hand in Figure has 30 points and is exceptionally strong.

Having explained this I must stress that there are all sorts of other factors that come into valuation, as you will find with experience. An undoubted disadvantage of the point-count is that it is so easy to apply. Players quickly gain facility with it and often use their notions of point-count as a substitute for thinking. I cannot emphasise too strongly that the point-count is to be used *only* as a rough and ready guide to the strength of a hand. As the auction proceeds other considerations arise and if you ignore these and remain faithful to the great god Points you will never become a good player.

The value of a hand might increase or decrease dramatically during the auction according to the bids made by your partner or opponents. A guarded king, for instance, could become a valuable winner if you are sure the ace is on your right.

Distributional Strength

We have seen that an average hand contains 10 points in honour cards. As we will see in Chapter Six, to open the bidding with one of a suit your hand needs to be at least a king or so above average. The hands in Figures 31 to 33 are all minimum openings.

Fig. 31

Fig. 32

Fig. 33

You will notice that each of these hands has about 13 points. But what about this next hand in Figure 34?

Fig. 34

Now there are only 11 points in high cards, scarcely over average. But the good six-card suit provides compensation for the lack of high cards—after all, you would expect to make at least six tricks in a heart contract all by yourself, which is more than you can say for the hand in Figure 31. In practice the rules are relaxed for hands with six-card suits, and it is enough to have 11 points in high cards to open on one of these.

The purpose of this example is to introduce the idea of **distributional strength**. The hand in Figure 34 is said to have distributional strength, in addition to its high-card strength.

It is convenient for beginners to use a point count for distribution as well as for high cards, and the simplest and most popular is:

For each card over four in a suit, add one point

So now we have the total point count (TPC) of a hand as the sum of the high-card points (HCP) and the distributional points (DP).

The Use of the Total Point Count

The importance of the TPC is that it helps the partnership to judge how high they can afford to bid in their best denomination. The table below shows the TPC required in the combined hands to make contracts at various levels.

The TPC Table
TPC for different levels of contract

Contract	TPC requirements	Zone
One No-Trump *or* Suit contract at Two level	21–22	
		I
Two No-Trumps *or* Suit contract at Three level	23–24	
Game contract in No-Trumps or major suit	25–26	II
Game in minor suit	28–29	III
Small Slam	33–34	IV
Grand Slam	37–38	V

There are five different zones shown in the table. Zone I is the part-score zone. Zone II is the No-Trump or major suit game zone. Zone III is the minor suit game zone. Zone IV is the Small Slam zone and Zone V the Grand Slam zone. Good bidding consists of determining as quickly as possible the correct denomination and correct zone for the combined hands of the partnership. How this is done we will see in the next chapters.

Chapter Five

No-Trump Openings and Responses

Opening Bid of One No-Trump
The classical opening bid of One No-Trump is made on a balanced hand with honours (preferably tenaces—see Chapter Two) in all four suits. A balanced hand is one with 4-3-3-3 or 4-4-3-2 shape. (A hand with its thirteen cards made up of four in one suit and three in each of the others is referred to as '4-3-3-3'). If the five-card suit is a minor, 5-3-3-2 shape is also permitted.

The strength of the hand should be 15-17 HCP. The hands in Figures 35 to 39 show typical opening bids on One No-Trump.

Fig. 35

Fig. 38

Fig. 36

Fig. 39

In contrast, the hands in Figures 40 to 42 each have some defect which makes them unsuitable.

Fig. 37

Fig. 40

Fig. 41

Fig. 42

The hand in Figure 40 is not strong enough (only 14 points) and would be opened One Club (see Chapter Six). The hand in Figure 41 has the right strength, but no tenaces and a weak doubleton, and again should be opened One Club. The hand in Figure 42 has the right strength but with a five-card major suit it is usually best to open that suit.

Notice that I said that the hand in Figure 40 was not strong enough. You might reasonably ask why not open all balanced hands with a No-Trump bid. After all, when you have a hand with honour cards in all the suits much the most likely final contract is in No-Trumps.

The answer to that question is that all No-Trump openings (and most other No-Trump bids) are *Limit Bids*. A Limit Bid is a bid that describes the strength of a hand to within a narrow range, normally of 2 points. The importance of a Limit Bid is that it puts the limit bidder's partner in command–he now knows the limit bidder's strength and by adding it to his own can work out the combined partnership strength. He can then decide which contract zone of the TPC Table the partnership are in, and make some appropriate bid.

When you make a limit bid you are approaching that ideal I mention in Chapter Four of laying your hand face up on the table, to put your partner in charge of the two hands. Our first examples of responding to limit bids are shown below in the

discussion on responding to the One No-Trump opening.

Opening Strength. While I recommend that you play a 15-17 No-Trump, several ranges are in use. What they have in common is that the range of strengths allowed is at most 3 points. Many English tournament players use a 12-14 point One No-Trump (referred to as a Weak No-Trump). Others may play a Weak No-Trump not vulnerable, but an intermediate (14-16) or strong (15-17 or 16-18) No-Trump vulnerable. The principles of bidding involved are the same in all cases.

Responding to One No-Trump

The first thing the responder should do is to add his strength to that of the opener, to determine which strength zone the partnership is in. Thus in Figure 43 you

Fig. 43

see that your 7 points added onto the opener's 15-17 means that the partnership has 22-24 points. That is not enough to move out of the part-score into the game zone. If the opener is maximum he may be able to make eight tricks in No-Trumps. But once you realise that there is no possibility of a game, you should endeavour to play at as low a level as possible. A part-score of 70 is little different from a part-score of 40; but if you play in Two No-Trumps and go one down you will have thrown away the chance of a 40 part-score.

Fig. 44

So on the hand in Figure 43 you pass One No-Trump.

Strengthen the hand, as in Figure 44. Now you know that the partnership has 26-28 points, enough to put you into the game zone but not enough for a slam. So you bid Three No-Trumps over your partner's One No-Trump.

Sometimes you are not in a position to make such a unilateral decision, as in in Figure 45.

Fig. 45

If the opener has 17 points you will have enough between the hands to put you in the game zone, but if he has only 15 points opposite your 9 it will be more prudent for you to stop in Two No-Trumps. So you bid Two No-Trumps over One No-Trump. This is an invitational bid – it says to your partner 'If you have a maximum we should have a play for Three No-Trumps; otherwise I don't think we should go any higher.'

In Figure 46 two possible hands for the opener are given:

Fig. 46

	Opener			Responder
(I)	♠ K 9 3		♠	A 8 4
	♥ K 8 2	W E	♥	Q J 3
	♦ A K J		♦	Q 10 6 2
	♣ J 10 7 3		♣	9 5 4
(II)	♠ K Q 3			
	♥ K 8 2			
	♦ A K J			
	♣ J 10 7 3			

On hand I the opener has a minimum (15 points) so he passes the raise to Two No-Trumps. On hand II he has 17 points, so he goes on to Three No-Trumps.

You can see that when the declarer has hand II opposite the responder's hand he can make nine tricks by playing on hearts as soon as he gains the lead. All the defence can take are three club tricks and the ace

of hearts. When the declarer has hand I the defence can attack spades to beat Three No-Trumps, but the declarer can still make Two No-Trumps by knocking out the ace of hearts.

Weakness Take-out. Sometimes when your partner opens One No-Trump you will hold a hand like that in Figure 47.

Fig. 47

Even counting extra distribution points you can see that you are still in the part-score zone. But it is not correct on this hand to pass. Say your partner had the hand in Figure 48.

Fig. 48

Now you would probably go down in One No-Trump with two spades an easy make.

The solution is to bid Two Spades, termed a **weakness take-out.** Note the difference between this bid and the invitational Two No-Trump bid. The weakness take-out is a **sign-off** bid: the opener must pass it.

Fig. 49

Fig. 50

The hands in Figures 49 and 50 show other examples of weakness take-out. On the hand in Figure 49 you bid Two Hearts and on that in Figure 50 Two Diamonds.

Fig. 51

Fig. 52

Fig. 53

used for another purpose (see below). So you just have to hope for the best in One No-Trump.

On stronger hands of the type in Figure 53 you may have enough to bid a game.

Again you insist on playing in spades, but now there ought to be a play for Four Spades, so you bid an immediate Four Spades over the opening One No-Trump.

The Forcing Take-out

Fig. 54

The hand in Figure 54 is worth game opposite an opening One No-Trump. Two possible hands for the opener are given in Figures 55 and 56.

Fig. 55

Fig. 56

On the hand in Figure 51 it is better to pass One No-Trump. The 5-3-3-2 shape is not really suitable for a weakness take-out. The hand in Figure 52 is suitable for a take-out into Two Clubs but that bid is

If the opener has the hand in Figure 55 opposite the hand in Figure 54, the best contract is Four Hearts. In that contract the declarer will be unlucky to lose more than one spade, one heart and one club. But

24

if the contract is Three No-Trumps a spade attack is likely to beat it.

However if the hand in Figure 56 is opposite the hand in Figure 54 the best contract is Three No-Trumps. Now the declarer has an easy nine tricks via two spades, two hearts, three diamonds and two clubs. But he will have to be lucky in Four Hearts not to lose a heart trick in addition to the ace, king of spades and ace of clubs.

The way the responder ensures that the partnership gets to the correct contract whichever of the above hands the opener holds is to respond Three Hearts to One No-Trump. This is a *forcing* bid: that is, the opener is not allowed to pass. In all bidding sequences a jump in a new suit below the game level is forcing to game. In this case the bid says 'Partner I have at least five hearts and a game-going hand. If you have support for my hearts raise me to Four Hearts. Otherwise bid Three No-Trumps.' When the opener has the hand in Figure 55 he will bid Four Hearts over Three Hearts, but on the hand in Figure 56 he bids Three No-Trumps.

One each of the hands in Figures 57 and 58 the responder should reply with Three Spades over an opening One No-Trump.

Fig. 57

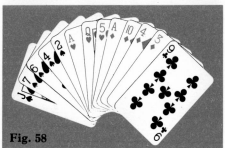
Fig. 58

The forcing take-out may also be the first step on a hand worth a slam.

If you hold a good hand and your partner opens the bidding you may envisage a slam but must still find the best contract.

Fig. 59

♠ A J 3 2		♠ 5
♥ K J 10 4	W E	♥ A Q 9 8 6
♦ K 4		♦ A J 6 2
♣ K 8 3		♣ A 7 4

An untutored but effective auction on the hands in Figure 59 is:

West	East
1NT	3 ♥
4 ♥	6 ♥

When East hears his partner open One No-Trump he realises that the combined partnership strength is near the slam zone. But he still starts with Three Hearts. West at this point does not realise that his partner has higher ambitions. With his heart support he dutifully raises. Now East could approach more slowly, but his bid of Six Hearts is certainly reasonable—he has *aces*, which are particularly important cards for slam contracts.

Playing in hearts East can ruff two diamonds in the West hand, thus making twelve tricks via ace of spades, five hearts in his own hand, ace and king of diamonds and two ruffs, and ace and king of clubs. All he has to be careful about is not to play off too many hearts before he has ruffed his losing diamonds. But in No-Trumps there is little chance of twelve tricks. Even if the diamond finesse succeeds that still only gives eleven tricks, as one of the defenders will control the fourth round of the suit.

The Stayman Convention
What about the hand in Figure 60 opposite a One No-Trump opening?

Fig. 60

You have enough strength to bid a game, and most of the time you wouldn't be far wrong if you just bid Three No-Trumps over One No-Trump. But if your partner holds the hand in Figure 61 you will find

Fig. 61

Fig. 63

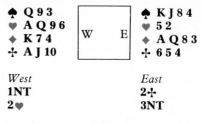

♠ Q 9 3		♠ K J 8 4
♥ A Q 9 6	W E	♥ 5 2
♦ K 7 4		♦ A Q 8 3
♣ A J 10		♣ 6 5 4

West	*East*
1NT	2♣
2♥	3NT

Fig. 64

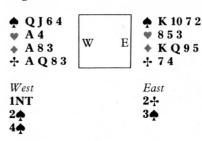

♠ Q J 6 4		♠ K 10 7 2
♥ A 4	W E	♥ 8 5 3
♦ A 8 3		♦ K Q 9 5
♣ A Q 8 3		♣ 7 4

West	*East*
1NT	2♣
2♠	3♠
4♠	

yourself losing the ace of spades and at least four heart tricks. Meanwhile a contract of Four Spades is a racing certainty.

Notice that you cannot bid Two Spades over One No-Trump. That would be a weakness take-out. Nor can you bid Three Spades, as that would show at least five spades. The solution is to use a **conventional bid** of Two Clubs over One No-Trump.

A conventional bid is a bid which has a codified meaning unrelated to the denomination of the bid. Any convention has to be agreed between the partners beforehand, but provided the opponents also know what the meaning is, it is quite permissible.

In this instance the Two Club bid has no relation to Clubs. It is a bid which asks the opener to bid a four-card major suit if he has one. Otherwise he bids Two Diamonds, another conventional bid, which simply denies a four-card major.

This use of Two Clubs as an enquiry is called the **Stayman convention**. Below are some examples of it in action.

Fig. 62

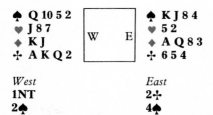

♠ Q 10 5 2		♠ K J 8 4
♥ J 8 7	W E	♥ 5 2
♦ K J		♦ A Q 8 3
♣ A K Q 2		♣ 6 5 4

West	*East*
1NT	2♣
2♠	4♠

The hands in Figure 62 are the hands in Figures 60 and 61 put together. East asks for a four-card major with Two Clubs. West obliges by showing his spades, and East raises to game.

In Figure 63 West's four-card major is in hearts. East is not interested in playing in that suit, so he just bids Three No-Trumps.

In Figure 64 East has not got enough strength to go to game if the opener is minimum. So he bids Two Clubs intending to bid Two No-Trumps if the opener does not have spades. When the opener shows four spades East makes an invitational raise to Three Spades, a bid analogous to the invitational raise to Two No-Trumps. West is maximum, and furthermore most of his strength is in Aces, so he is happy to oblige.

Opening Bid of Two No-Trumps
An opening of Two No-Trumps shows a balanced hand of strength 20-22 points.

Fig. 65

Figure 65 shows a typical Two No-Trump opening.

Again it is the responder who is in charge. He knows the opener's strength and approximate shape and it is up to him to place the final contract. His options are:
i) Pass. This he must do on any hand of less than about 4 points.

ii) Bid Three No-Trumps. This shows a hand of 4–10 points with no interest in playing in a major suit.

iii) Bid Three of a major suit to ask his partner to choose between Four of a major and Three No-Trumps. Note that this is analagous to the Three of a major over One No-Trump. A typical hand might be as in Figure 66.

Fig. 67

Fig. 66

Responder bids Three Spades over Two No-Trumps, and passes if the opener rebids Three No-Trumps.

iv) Bid Four of a major on 4 or more points and a six-card suit.

With the hand in Figure 67 responder bids Four Hearts over his partner's Two No-Trumps.

v) Bid Three Clubs (Stayman) to ask for a four-card major.

Fig. 68

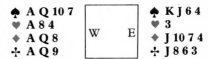

♠ A Q 10 7		♠ K J 6 4
♥ A 8 4		♥ 3
♦ A Q 8	W E	♦ J 10 7 4
♣ A Q 9		♣ J 8 6 3

On the deal in Figure 68 the bidding goes:

West	*East*
2NT	**3♣**
3♠	**4♠**

If East's spades and hearts were reversed he would bid Three No-Trumps over Three Spades.

Chapter Six

The Opening Bid in a Suit

Only a small proportion of hands qualify for an opening bid of One No-Trump. The majority of opening bids are made at the One level in a suit.

Strength

The opening of one of a suit is made on hands with a Total Point Count in the 13–20 range. Some 12-point hands may also be opened.

Immediately we see a difference from the One No-Trump opening. An opening bid of say One Heart can be made on a variety of different shapes, with a wide range of strength. Accordingly it is not until later on in the auction that the opener will be able to define his hand more exactly. After an opening of One No-Trump the responder already knows most of what there is to know about the opener's hand. Before going into details of the choice of opening bid I will set the scene with some straightforward examples. The easiest hands to deal with are those with only one suit of more than four cards (referred to as 'one-suiters'). If the long suit has five cards or more, it is invariably correct to open the bidding with one of the long suit. In Chapter Four I gave the hands in Figures 31 and 34 as instances of minimum opening bids and these hands are repeated overleaf as Figures 69 and 70.

Fig. 69

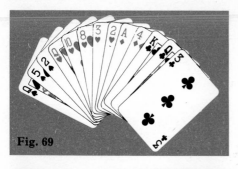

Fig. 73

Fig. 70

Fig. 74

The hand in Figure 69 has a TPC of 14, counting 1 for the fifth heart. It is opened with One Heart. The hand in Figure 70 has a TPC of 13, that is 11 in high cards and 1 each for the fifth and sixth hearts. It too is opened with One Heart.

What would you do with the hands in Figures 71 to 74?

The hand in Figure 71 adds up to 18 TPC with 16 in high cards and 2 for the six-card spade suit. More than a minimum

but still a One Spade opener. The hand in Figure 72 has a TPC of 20, and is a maximum One Club opening. But the hand in Figure 73 is not strong enough to warrant opening, and you should pass.

The hand in Figure 74 has two five-card suits, so picks up a distributional point for each of them. It is the first hand on which we had more than one long suit; this hand introduces an important topic that is discussed in the next section.

The Choice of Opening Bid
When you open the bidding with one of a suit as dealer or second in hand, you make a commitment to bid again if your partner replies in a different suit. This is not a rule of bridge, it is simply an agreement between the partners. In a sense it is a bidding *convention*, in the same way that the Stayman Two Club bid we saw in Chapter Five is a convention. The notion is known as the ***Approach Forcing Principle***.

You will notice I said as dealer or second in hand—if you are third or fourth in hand it follows that your partner has already passed, and in that case you are not obliged to bid again over his reply.

So when you open the bidding in the first two positions you not only have to decide on what to open, but also on what to rebid over any of your partner's possible replies. You should never make that first bid until you have made up your mind on your second bid. A player who picks up

Fig. 71

Fig. 72

28

his hand and briskly opens One Heart and then goes into a long trance when his partner replies One Spade is admitting that he has not carried out this process properly.

The rebid problem is discussed in more detail in Chapter Eight. In this chapter we will only be considering it in relation to the opening bid, and in particular with respect to *minimum* openings. The choice of openings on stronger hands is usually easier.

One-suited Hands

The easiest types of hands to deal with are those with one long suit. The rule is simple enough here. With a minimum opening bid (up to about 15 points) you simply repeat your suit.

Fig. 75

With the hand in Figure 75, open One Spade, and rebid Two Spades whatever partner's reply.

Fig. 76

With the hand in Figure 76, open One Heart and rebid Two Hearts. Normally you will find that the rebid shows a six-card or good five-card suit, though at times it is unavoidable on a weaker five. For example in Figure 77 there is no option but to rebid Two Hearts over a response of Two Clubs or Two Diamonds, but over a response of One Spade you would thankfully rebid One No-Trump. You are not strong enough in clubs, diamonds or spades to support any of these suits.

Fig. 77

Two-suited Hands

A two-suited hand is one with two suits of at least four cards each. If both the suits are four-carders, the hand is often better treated as balanced.

When the suits are of unequal length you open with the longer and show the shorter on the next round if possible.

Fig. 78

With Figure 78 open One Spade and rebid Two Hearts over a response of Two in a minor.

Fig. 79

With Figure 79 open One Spade and rebid Two Diamonds over Two Clubs. But over a Two Heart response you have to suppress your diamonds and rebid Two Spades. As we will see in Chapter Eight, your hand is not strong enough to rebid at the three level with Three Diamonds.

Now in Figure 80 you have a six-card suit and a four-card suit. When the six-card suit is strong and the four-carder weak, it is

Fig. 80

correct to suppress the second suit. You rebid Two Spades over a response of Two Clubs or Two Diamonds, as if your hand were a one-suiter.

But with Figure 81 you open One Spade

Fig. 81

and rebid Two Hearts.

With equal length suits the technique varies according to whether they are *touching* or not. Suits are said to be touching when they are adjacent in bidding rank. Thus spades and hearts are touching, as are hearts and diamonds, diamonds and clubs.

With *touching suits* open the higher and rebid in the lower.

Fig. 82

With Figure 82 open One Heart and rebid Two Diamonds. Why not open One Diamond and rebid Two Hearts, you may ask. After all, the diamonds are considerably stronger than the hearts. The reason you open One Heart is for economy – the One
30   Heart bid saves space.

Say your partner had a weak hand with a five-card spade suit, and that he preferred your diamonds to your hearts. Then compare the following two sequences:

1)	*West*	*East*
	1♥	**1♠**
	2♦	**Pass**
2)	**1♦**	**1♠**
	2♥	**3♦**

In the second sequence your partner has had to go to the Three level merely to express the fact that he likes your diamonds better than your hearts. In the first sequence he could express that preference at the Two level, either by passing Two Diamonds or by bidding Two Hearts over Two Diamonds. So the effect of opening One Heart in Figure 82 is to keep the bidding low – a good general principle.

If you have grasped that point, you won't

Fig. 83

Fig. 84

Fig. 85

have any trouble with the hands in Figures 83 to 85.

With the hand in Figure 83 you open One Spade and rebid Two Hearts, and with that in Figure 84 open One Diamond and rebid Two Clubs. Figure 85 is our first example of a hand with two four-card suits. When the suits are as strong as this, you again treat the hand as a two-suiter, opening One Heart and rebidding Two Diamonds.

With *non-touching* suits the issue is more complicated. With spades and clubs it is best to open the clubs. With spades and diamonds or hearts and clubs, open with the major suit.

Fig. 86

Fig. 87

Fig. 88

With Figure 86 open One Club and rebid One Spade. With Figure 87 open One Spade and with Figure 88 One Heart. If partner responds Two Hearts in Figure 87, or Two Diamonds in Figure 88 you would have to rebid your second suit at the Three level. These hands are not strong enough

for that so you just rebid the major suit. But if partner responds in clubs in Figure 87 or in spades in Figure 88, you will be able to show the second suit.

The important thing to note is that if there is a danger of one suit being shut out, it is better to make certain of showing the major suit. With the hand in Figure 86 you can afford to open One Club as no response will force you to bid the spades at an uncomfortable level.

Three-suited Hands

Three-suited hands either have five cards in one suit and four in each of two others, or have three four-card suits and a singleton.
4-4-4-1. If you consider what you are going to rebid, you won't find the choice of opening difficult. The general rule is 'usually the suit below the singleton'. You never open the suit above the singleton.

Fig. 89

Fig. 90

In Figure 89 you open One Diamond, intending to rebid One Spade over One Heart; in Figure 90 you open One Club, intending to bid One Heart over One Diamond.

Exceptions occur when the suit below the singleton is weak, and when the three suits are touching, as in Figures 91 to 93. With the hand in Figure 91 you will still have an easy rebid if you open One Club. In Figure 92 it would not be wrong to open One Heart, but One Diamond leaves room

Fig. 91

Fig. 92

Fig. 93

for partner to bid hearts and still gives you a satisfactory rebid of Two Clubs if he responds One Spade. In Figure 93 again it is not a mistake to open One Spade (in this instance spades are considered to be the 'suit below the singleton'), but One Heart is more flexible.

5-4-4-0. Now you always open with the five-card suit unless it is so weak that you consider it the equivalent of a four-card suit.

Fig. 94

Fig. 95

With Figure 94 you open One Spade, and just have to rebid Two Spades if partner responds Two Hearts. With Figure 95 it would be too painful to suppress both your major suits after One Diamond—Two Clubs; you open One Heart, mentally treating the hand as though it was 4-4-4-1 with a singleton club.

Balanced Hands

As we saw from Chapter Five, hands which have 4-3-3-3 or 4-4-3-2 distribution are described as 'balanced'. Hands which are 5-3-3-2 are often treated as balanced.

The general idea with balanced hands is to open with One of a suit and rebid in No-Trumps, or to open One No-Trump. This section is concerned with hands which for one reason or another are not suitable for an opening One No-Trump bid.

Fig. 96

Fig. 97

With Figure 96 you are not strong enough to open One No-Trump, so you open One

Club and rebid One No-Trump over any one level response. With Figure 97 you again open One Club. If partner responds One Spade you rebid One No-Trump, but if partner responds One Diamond, One Heart is a more satisfactory rebid, in view of your good heart suit and weak spades.

Fig. 98

With Figure 98 you open One Diamond and rebid One No-Trump over One Heart or One Spade. A problem arises if partner responds Two Clubs. To rebid Two No-Trumps you require rather more strength than a minimum opening (see Chapter Eight) so now you have to rebid Two Diamonds.

Fig. 99

Fig. 100

With Figure 99 your first thoughts are probably to open One Spade. But if your partner responds at the two level you will have no decent rebid–Two Spades would show a five-card suit and Two No-Trumps would show more strength. The solution to

this dilemma is to open *all* weak 4-3-3-3 hands with One Club, with the intention of rebidding One No-Trump over partner's response.

So in Figure 99 you open One Club and rebid One No-Trump over One Diamond or One Heart; the treatment is similar for Figure 100.

You will observe that we now have an exception to the general rule that the opening of one of a suit guarantees at least four cards in the suit. An opening of One Club followed by a rebid of One No-Trump *may* be based on a three-card club suit. Such an opening is called a **Prepared Club**–it *prepares* the opener's rebid.

Third and Fourth Hand Openings
If the opener's partner has already passed, the obligation for the opener to rebid no longer exists. So now it is correct for the opener to bid his best suit.

Fig. 101

First in hand Figure 101 would have to be opened with a slightly uncomfortable One Club. But in third or fourth seat One Spade is the correct bid–the opener has heard his partner pass, so he knows that the partnership cannot have enough strength to make a game. So the opener will pass anything his partner says, and he takes this opportunity to show his best suit.

Fig. 102

Again first in hand the bid in Figure 102 would be One Club, preparing for a bid of

One Heart over One Diamond and One No-Trump over One Spade. But in third seat One Heart is a more aggressive move – you intend to bid One No-Trump over One Spade, and to pass a response of Two Diamonds.

The removal of the rebid obligation can make some hands worth an opening that would have to be passed in the first two positions.

Fig. 103

The hand in Figure 103 isn't worth a bid as dealer. But third in hand not much harm will come to you if you open One Heart, and if your opponents buy the contract you will have shown your partner a good lead.

Light Openings – More Advanced Notions

You may remember that I issued some dire warnings about the misuse of the point count when I first introduced the idea. So far I haven't enlarged on these warnings,

Fig. 104

Fig. 105

but by now you may be ready for some more discussion on valuation. By way of illustration I give below some examples to show how these aspects of valuation affect marginal opening bids.

Rebidding. A factor in marginal opening bids is the rebid. Often a hand is worth an opening bid if it has a good rebid, and not otherwise.

Both hands in Figures 104 and 105 have a TPC of 12 points. Both are near to opening strength, as their high cards are concentrated (see below) and they have controls. But Figure 104 is not an opening bid because it does not have a decent rebid – after an opening of One Spade the opener would have to rebid Two Spades over a red suit response, thus suppressing one of the good features of his hand. Figure 105 is definitely worth an opening bid, as the opener will be able to show both his suits at a low level.

Strength in Long Suits. It is better to have your strength in your long suits. The reason for that is that high cards in your long suits are helping to make the small cards into tricks; if the high cards are in short suits they are not being used to develop long-card winners.

Fig. 106

Fig. 107

The hand in Figure 106 is not worth an opening bid because it has few of its points in the long suit. Figure 107 has that

desirable feature, and should be opened.

Concentration of Strength. In a way this is another aspect of the long suit strength idea.

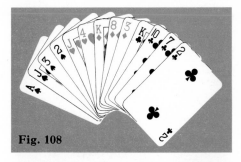

Fig. 108

Fig. 109

Figure 109 is a better hand than Figure 108. The jack of hearts by itself is of nebulous worth; it may or may not help to produce a trick, depending on partner's hand. But the K 8 3 diamond combination of Figure 108 is definitely strengthened by the substitution of the jack for the eight. So in view of the convenient rebid it would be reasonable to open in Figure 109, while Figure 108 is a clear pass.

Devaluing Honours in Short Suits. The J x combination in Figure 108 might prove worthless. The same goes for doubleton queens. And singleton honours are never worth their full point count. They have to be played on the first round of the suit willy-nilly, and so are much less flexible than honours backed up by small cards. I

Fig. 110

Fig. 111

Fig. 112

advise deducting one point for any singleton honour holding.

Figure 110 is not worth opening because of the singleton king and poor hearts. Figure 111 is a distinct improvement, well worth a One Heart opening. Figure 112 has its honours in its short suits and should be passed.

Intermediate Cards. So far we have only considered the high card strength in terms of honour cards. But tens and nines can be

Fig. 113

Fig. 114

important as well, particularly when they occur in combination with honours. Figure 113 is considerably stronger than the high-card count of 14 might suggest. It certainly would not be wrong to open it with a 15-17 One No-Trump. Figure 114 has as many points in picture cards, yet is not much more than a minimum One Club opener.

Higher Openings

There is not room in a book of this length to discuss these in any great detail.

Forcing Openings

Sometimes you may hold a hand so strong that you cannot risk your partner passing your opening bid. So you have to make a forcing opening bid. Nowadays most players use some type of **Two Club** force. An opening of Two Clubs is conventional and forcing to game; the responder must reply. On the second round of the auction the opener starts to describe his hand by bidding his best suit.

Openings of Two in the other suits are played in three distinct styles:

Acol Twos. In the UK an opening of Two Diamonds, Hearts or Spades shows a powerful hand with a strong suit. These bids are forcing for one round of bidding.

Strong Twos. In this method, now dying out, any Two bid is natural to the extent that it shows that suit, but is forcing to game.

Weak Twos. In this method a Two opening other than Two Clubs shows a six-card suit and a weak hand with 7–11 points.

Pre-emptive Openings

Openings at the Three level and above are **pre-emptive**. They show weak hands with at least seven of the suit named, and they are bids designed to make it awkward for the opposition to enter the auction.

Chapter Seven

Responding to One of a Suit

After an opening bid of one of a suit, the **responder** has several options.
i) He can pass.
ii) He can **raise** the opener's suit—that is he can make a higher call in the same suit. In general, raises are Limit Bids.
iii) He can respond in No-Trumps. As for opening bids in No-Trumps, these responses are Limit Bids.
iv) He can respond in a new suit.

Responder's Pass

The minimum strength required to respond to the opener's bid of One of a suit is **5 points**. The logic of this is that if the opener has his maximum of 20 points and

Fig. 115

Fig. 116

the responder 5, the partnership may well be able to make a game; hence if the responder passes on his 5 points his side may miss a game. But when the responder has less than 5 points he knows there will be no game, so he does not raise false hopes in his partner by making a response.

The hands in Figures 115 to 118 are maximum passes over an opening of One Heart: improve any of them by a point or so and they would be worth a bid.

Raises of Opener's Suit
Single Raise

If the responder has length in a major suit opened by his partner, it is usually correct to *raise* that suit. One of the most important functions of the early rounds of bidding is to search for a *major-suit fit* – that is, to find a major suit in which the partnership have at least seven and usually at least eight cards. Once an eight-card fit has been found it is rare that the partnership will play the contract in another denomination. All they will be concerned with from then on is the level of the final contract.

The raise from One to Two is the weakest raise, and is made on hands with about *6–10 points*. After a major suit opening the responder needs three trumps headed by an honour, or any four trumps, to give the single raise.

In addition to high-card strength, the

responder like the opener takes account of his distributional strength. On the whole the most valuable distributional feature of a *supporting* hand (that is a hand that raises its partner's suit) is its shortages in side suits. Look at the deals in Figures 119 and 120.

Fig. 119

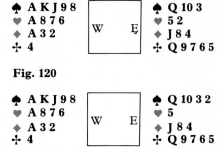

Fig. 120

♠ A K J 9 8   ♠ Q 10 3 2
♥ A 8 7 6   W   E   ♥ 5
♦ A 3 2   ♦ J 8 4
♣ 4   ♣ Q 9 7 6 5

The difference between the East hands is simply that in Figure 120 the two of hearts has been changed into the two of spades. According to the valuation for distribution that I describe in Chapter Four both East hands have one point for distribution, for the fifth club. Yet in support of the West hand, the East hand in Figure 120 is worth one to two tricks more than that in Figure 119. On the second deal West would have a good chance of ruffing his three losing hearts in the East hand. On the first deal he would only be able to ruff two of them; if the defence led trumps and then played trumps when they got in with a heart West would end up with two fewer tricks than in Figure 120.

The lesson to be learned here is the importance of *short* suits in the supporting hand, particularly when combined with trump length. A reasonably satisfactory way of quantifying distributional strength in support is the following:

With four card support :
add 1 point for each side suit doubleton
add 2 points for each side singleton
add 3 points for each side suit void
With three card support :
1 point for a singleton
2 points for a void

Using this scheme the East hand in Figure 119 would be worth just 5 points in support (no extra points for distribution are awarded for a hand with only three-card support). The East hand in Figure 120 is worth a total of 7 points – 5 in high cards, plus 2 for the singleton heart in combination with four trumps.

Examples. West opens One Heart. On each of the hands in Figures 121 to 123 East should raise to Two Hearts.

Fig. 121

Fig. 122

Fig. 123

Fig. 124

responding in a new suit. On the next three hands (Figures 125 to 127) a raise of One Diamond to Two Diamonds is correct.

Fig. 125

Fig. 126

Fig. 127

Figure 121 does not get any points for distribution, though the possibility of a spade ruff may increase its value. Figure 122 is awarded 3 points for distribution, and accordingly is valued at 7 points. Figure 123 gets 1 point for distribution and so is also valued at 7 points.

Some players might respond One Spade on hands like Figure 123. That is quite wrong. As soon as you know there is a major suit fit you should let your partner into the secret by an immediate raise.

After a minor suit opening the raise is normally based on four-card support.

The hand in Figure 124 is just Figure 121 with the diamonds and hearts reversed. But the correct bid over a One Diamond opening is One Heart, not Two Diamonds. You will see why in the section on

Double Raise

The requirements for a double raise are **10–12 points**, and at least four-card trump support.

As before, if you have support for your partner's major suit and the requisite strength, you look no further for your bid.

Fig. 128

Fig. 129

Fig. 130

Fig. 131

Fig. 132

to give a double raise immediately. In Figure 131 you respond Two Diamonds over One Spade, and in Figure 132 One Spade over One Heart.

After a minor suit opening the double raise should normally contain at least 10 high-card points. This is because the partnership may end up in Three No-Trumps, and points counted for short suits won't be much use in that contract. Also it is normally better to respond in a four-card major if you have one.

If in Figure 133 the hearts and diamonds were reversed you would certainly raise an opening One Heart to Three. But with the hand as it is, it is prudent only to bid Two Diamonds over a One Diamond opener. Figure 134 is a typical One Diamond–Three Diamond raise. With Figure 135 it is better to bid One Spade over One Diamond.

In the USA the raise to three is sometimes played as showing a stronger

Fig. 133

Figure 128 is worth a raise to three whichever major partner opens. It has 11 high-card points and scores one more for the doubleton club in conjunction with four trumps. Figure 129 is a typical Three Heart bid over One Heart—it has 9 high-card points and 2 for the singleton diamond. Figure 130 is worth a raise of One Spade to Three Spades—9 high-card points and 2 more for the two doubletons.

With three-card support it is not correct

Fig. 134

Fig. 135

Fig. 138

hand, 13-16 points. After this raise (referred to as a 'Forcing raise') the bidding is not allowed to die below the game level. The method is not used so much nowadays, and I strongly recommend that you use the 'Limit Raise' style that I describe here.

The Game Raise in a Major

Again there is a dichotomy of styles between the UK and the USA. In the USA the bid shows around 10-12 points with good major support and unbalanced distribution. In the UK the game raise is made both on this type of hand and on hands which are rather stronger in high cards and weaker in distribution, in all being worth around 13–15 points in support.

Fig. 139

Figures 138 and 139 illustrate the difference between the two styles. In the UK Figure 138 is a raise to Four Hearts over an opening One Heart, and Figure 139 is a raise to Four Spades over One Spade. The American style is to respond either Two Diamonds or Two No-Trumps (see below) in Figure 138, and follow with Four Hearts on the next round. In Figure 139 the Americans respond Two Diamonds and follow with Four Spades.

Fig. 136

Fig. 140

Fig. 137

Fig. 141

Both of the hands in Figures 136 and 137 are worth a raise from One Spade to Four Spades in either style, each hand having the requisite 10 points with good spades and an unbalanced distribution.

40

The Raise to Four or Five of a Minor

These raises are played in a pre-emptive style on both sides of the Atlantic. They occur rarely. The hand in Figure 140 qualifies for a Four Club bid over an opening One Club.

A jump to Five needs an even more shapely hand.

In Figure 141 jump to Five Clubs over One Club.

No-Trump Responses

In the same way that it is desirable to open One No-Trump if you have a suitable hand, or to raise your partner's suit if you have the qualifications, the response in no-trumps is a *good* bid. As always, making a limit bid very much simplifies the subsequent auction.

No-trump responses, like no-trump openings, are made on balanced hands with honours in the unbid suits. The ideal holding in the opener's suit is two or three cards – usually there is a better bid available if the responder is short in the opener's suit.

The Response of One No-Trump

The response of One No-Trump shows 6-9 points and no four-card major biddable at the one level.

Fig. 142

Fig. 143

Figure 142 is an ideal One No-Trump response to One Heart. Over One Spade

Fig. 144

the three trumps combined with the ruffing value in Hearts would make Two Spades a better bid. Figure 143 is not quite so suitable a One No-Trump over One Spade, but the hand lacks the strength to bid at the two level. Figure 144 again is not ideal, but One No-Trump is still the best response over One Spade despite the singleton in partner's suit.

Fig. 145

Fig. 146

In Figure 145 the response over One Heart is One Spade, so that the partnership will not miss a spade fit. Some zealots recommend the same bid on Figure 146, but the more practical response is One No-Trump.

The Response of Two No-Trumps

Here we have another division of styles between the UK and the USA. In the UK the bid shows a balanced 11-12 points.

Figures 147 to 149 overleaf show three such hands.

Fig. 147

Fig. 148

Fig. 149

In Figure 147 respond Two No-Trumps over any opening of one in a suit. That is a better bid than raising a minor to the three level. In Figure 148 bid One Heart over a minor, Two No-Trumps over One Spade. In Figure 149 bid One Spade over any lower One bid.

In the USA the Two No-Trump bid shows 13-15 points. If the responder replies Two No-Trumps, it follows that the partnership must have enough strength for

Fig. 150

42

game, and so the bid is forcing to game. Figure 150 is a typical example of an American-style Two No-Trump response to One Spade. But if the responder has already passed, it follows that he cannot have more than 12 points, so now the Two No-Trump bid is played in the British style.

The Response of Three No-Trumps
This is not such a 'good' bid as the One No-Trump and Two No-Trump responses, as it consumes too much bidding space. The British style is to play it as showing 13-16 points, and precisely 4-3-3-3 distribution. The American style is similar, but now the bid shows 16-17 points.

Fig. 151

Fig. 152

Britons and Americans alike should respond Two Clubs to One Spade in Figure 151. To bid Three No-Trumps something like the hand in Figure 152 is needed.

The Response in a New Suit
The response in a new suit is an unlimited bid, at any rate at the upper end of the range. The responder should only reply in a new suit if he has no clear limit bid. In a good partnership, the fact that the responder bids a new suit implies that he *cannot make* a suitable limit bid.

Response at the One Level
If your partner opens One Club, it is

correct to respond One Heart on each of the hands in Figures 153 to 155.

Fig. 153

Fig. 154

Fig. 155

Those of you who may have some passing acquaintance with the older methods might be inclined to reply One No-Trump ('negative partner') on either Figures 154 or 155. But that would risk the partnership missing a four-four major suit fit, the most important of the eight-card fits. Look at the lay-out in Figure 156.

Fig. 156

♠ 10 6 5		♠ 3 2
♥ A Q 3 2	W E	♥ K J 8 6
♦ J 8 3		♦ A K 4
♣ Q 5 4		♣ A K J 9

East opens One Club and if West responds One No-Trump East will have enough to bid Three No-Trumps. He will have no reason to bid Two Hearts, as West's reply of One No-Trump denied holding four hearts. In Three No-Trumps East-West may easily lose the first five or six tricks in spades.

But if West replies One Heart, East raises to Four Hearts, and West makes ten tricks in comfort.

Responding at the Two Level
To respond at the Two level the responder needs rather more strength, around 9 to 10 points at least.

Fig. 157

Fig. 158

With the hand in Figure 157 you would respond One Heart to One of a minor, but over One Spade you are not strong enough to bid Two Hearts. So you have to bid One No-Trump. Figure 158 is about a minimum for a response of Two Hearts.

The Jump Take-out
If the responder has a good suit and about 16 points or more, it is best for him to jump

Fig. 159

Fig. 160

one round of bidding immediately. That establishes a game-forcing situation, and enables the bidding to proceed slowly thereafter. So the jump take-out while consuming an extra round of bidding early on often has the paradoxical effect of saving space.

With Figure 159 respond Two Spades to One of a minor or One Heart. With Figure 160 respond Two Hearts to one of a minor, Three Hearts to One Spade.

Chapter Eight
The Later Rounds of the Auction

As the auction goes on each player finds out more about his partner's hand. And if one of the players is not in a position to place the final contract, he should be striving to define his own hand, in particular with a limit bid, so that his partner can make the final decision.

The Opener's First Rebid
These notions are illustrated by the problems faced by the opener at his second turn.

Rebidding Over Responder's Limit Bid
The opener is now in a position to judge the likely final contract. If he realises that there is not enough for a game he should sign off. Clearly the most obvious sign-off is

to **pass** the responder's bid, as in Figure 161.

You open One Spade, responder replies either One No-Trump or Two Spades. You have little more than a minimum, and adding that to responder's known 6-9 or 6-10 points you can see that there cannot be enough for a game. So you decide to pass.

Fig. 162

In Figure 162 you open One Spade and your partner bids One No-Trump. You have not enough strength for a game, but even so One No-Trump will probably not be the best contract. So you bid Two Spades, again a sign-off. Compare this sequence with the weakness take-out sequence One No-Trump–Two Spades

Fig. 161

which is discussed in Chapter Five. You would also bid Three Spades over a response of Two No-Trumps in Figure 163.

Fig. 163

Now after One Spade–One No-Trump you know there is no game. But the hand will probably play better in a suit, so you remove One No-Trump into Two Diamonds and pass any further bid from your partner. The Two Diamond bid, a change of suit, has a higher upper limit of strength than the simple Two Spade rebid, and would also be in order with the hand in Figure 164.

Fig. 164

After One Spade–One No-Trump you bid Two Diamonds. If your partner passes that there won't be a game in the hand, but if he bids Two Spades you can try Two No-Trumps showing 16-17 points.

Trial Bids. Sometimes after a single raise the opener will have a good hand which

Fig. 165

might make game if his partner has a fit. The dealer opens One Heart with the hand in Figure 165 and is raised to Two Hearts. He has a good hand, and there may be a play for game, but it rather depends where his partner's high cards are, so the opener now rebids Three Diamonds, a *trial bid*. Since if all he were interested in was a part score he would clearly pass Two Hearts, the responder realises that the Three Diamond bid is a try for game. Further, the Three Diamond bid says 'Partner if you can help me in Diamonds bid game. Otherwise sign-off in Three Hearts.'

With the hand in Figure 166 the responder co-operates with the game try because his points are in diamonds.

Fig. 166

Put this hand opposite Figure 165 and you see that there are ten tricks and only three losers in a contract of Four Hearts. But if the responder holds the hand in Figure 167

Fig. 167

he recognises his diamond holding as unhelpful, and he signs off in Three Hearts. And if your partner happens to hold the hand shown in Figure 165, even that contract could go down.

Good holdings for the responder in the opener's trial-bid suit are K Q x, K x, A x, Q x. Medium holdings are Q x x, x x. The worst holdings are x x x, J x x, or four small cards: x x x x.

Sometimes the opener may have the type of hand in Figure 168.

Fig. 168

Fig. 170

Fig. 171

He opens One Heart and hears his partner respond One No-Trump. If his partner has 8 or 9 points there will be enough strength between the hands to try for Three No-Trumps. But if his partner has a minimum 6, then the final contract shouldn't be higher than Two No-Trumps. The solution is for the opener to raise to Two No-Trumps, which invites the responder to bid Three No-Trumps if he is maximum. Compare the sequence with the 1NT-2NT sequence in Chapter Five.

Rebidding Over Responder's Change of Suit

If the responder has replied in a new suit (sometimes referred to as a 'change of suit') then little is known about his strength. Again the opener's first priority is to limit himself if possible. All of the following bids are *limited*:
a) Rebid of opener's suit.
b) Rebid in No-Trumps.
c) Raise of responder's suit.

Bids of a new suit (i.e. the third suit mentioned in the auction) by the opener on the second round have a rather wider strength range.

When the opener makes one of the limit bids mentioned above, he must bid at a level appropriate to his strength:
a) Minimum openings (12-15 points) rebid One No-Trump, give a single raise, or rebid his suit at the minimum level.
b) Intermediate openings (16-18 points)

jump the bidding to Two No-Trumps, give a double raise or make a jump rebid in suit.
c) Strong openings (19-20 points) make a game bid.

On each of the hands in Figures 169 to 171 the opener opens One Diamond and hears the response from his partner One Spade.

In Figure 169 opener rebids One No-Trump, in Figure 170 Two Spades, in Figure 171 Two Diamonds.

Again in Figures 172 to 174 the sequence starts One Diamond–One Spade.

In Figure 172 the opener rebids Two No-Trumps to show that he is considerably better than a minimum, but not quite worth game if the responder is dead minimum; in Figure 173 he bids Three Spades, and in Figure 174 Three Diamonds. To make the jump rebid of his own suit the opener should have a strong six-card suit with two of the top three honours, as well as 16-18 points.

Fig. 169

Fig. 172

Fig. 173

Fig. 174

Examples of game-going hands are shown in Figures 175 and 176. The sequence starts One Club–One Heart.

Fig. 175

Fig. 176

In Figure 175 the opener rebids Three No-Trumps and in Figure 176 Four Hearts. (In the USA many experts would still only rebid Two No-Trumps with the hand in Figure 175, in effect making the bid forcing.) In some expert circles the jump to Four Hearts is used to show a hand with

more distribution and less shape (compare with the One Spade–Four Spade bid). But you won't go far wrong in bidding Four Hearts in Figure 176.

After a response at the Two level most of the responder's bids follow a similar pattern, with the exception that a rebid of Two No-Trumps now only shows around 15-16 points, and a Three No-Trump rebid about 17-18 points.

Opener's Rebid in a New Suit

It is not always possible for the opener to limit his hand on the second round, and so he may continue to describe his hand by bidding another suit. Figure 177 is an example, with its follow-up.

Fig. 177

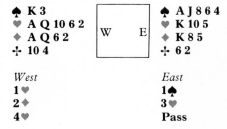

♠ K 3   ♠ A J 8 6 4
♥ A Q 10 6 2   ♥ K 10 5
♦ A Q 6 2   ♦ K 8 5
♣ 10 4   ♣ 6 2

West	*East*
1♥	1♠
2♦	3♥
4♥	Pass

On the second round West cannot limit his hand effectively, so bids Two Diamonds to show his second suit. East has reasonable support for both hearts and diamonds, but he prefers hearts (a) because that is a major suit, (b) because it is the opener's first suit and as such likely to be longer. So East makes a preference bid into hearts. But with his 11 points he knows the partnership must be near to a game, so he makes the encouraging jump preference bid of Three Hearts. West could pass that, but he is better than a minimum and has his side king in his partner's suit. So he bids Four Hearts, a contract that would be unlucky to fail.

Fig. 178

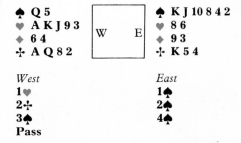

♠ Q 5   ♠ K J 10 8 4 2
♥ A K J 9 3   ♥ 8 6
♦ 6 4   ♦ 9 3
♣ A Q 8 2   ♣ K 5 4

West	*East*
1♥	1♠
2♣	2♠
3♠	4♠
Pass	

Again (Figure 178) West shows his second suit on his first rebid. East only has three card support for clubs (on the whole the responder should only aim to play in the opener's second suit if he has four-card support) but he has a good spade suit, so he rebids his spades. This is not a strong bid; however it does promise a reasonable six-card suit. West's Q x is sufficient to support a rebid suit, so he feels his hand is worth a raise to Three Spades. East with his fitting king of clubs has enough to go on to Four Spades.

Fig. 179

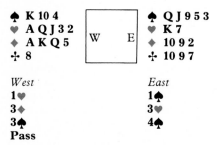

West	East
1♥	1♠
3♦	3♥
3♠	4♠
Pass	

In Figure 179 we have an example of a jump take-out by the opener. When West hears his partner respond One Spade he knows there will be a game in the hand somewhere, but for the moment he does not know in what denomination. He dare not bid Two Diamonds for fear East would

pass. So he establishes a game-forcing sequence by jumping to Three Diamonds.

While 10 9 x is not particularly good support, East would have passed a Two Diamond rebid. But now he is forced to bid, and the most flexible call is Three Hearts, often referred to as 'false preference' in that East has more diamonds than hearts. Over Three Hearts West offers spades as a possible contract with his Three Spade bid, and East is happy to co-operate.

The Reverse

In the following two sequences the opener makes a bid which forces the responder to give preference at the three level:

	West	East
1)	1♦	1♥
	2♥	3♦
2)	1♠	2♦
	3♣	3♠

In neither case has the responder promised extra strength, so it follows that for the partnership to be safe the opener must have more than a minimum. The Two Heart and Three Club bids are called **reverse bids**, and show at least 16-17 points.

Sequences involving reverses are rather complicated, and you will have to wait until you are more experienced to go any deeper into them.

Chapter Nine

Elements of Dummy Play

The most important quality required by a bridge player is the ability to think clearly. Often in the bidding or when you are defending a hand you may be taken slightly off-balance. But when you are playing the dummy that should never happen. You are in charge, and you can take your time.

Nowhere is this more important than at the first trick. When the opening lead has been made and your partner has put down

the dummy, *don't* play until you have formed a plan of campaign. The rest of this chapter describes some of the weapons you can use in the campaign.

Unblocking

Often you have hands where you have enough tricks, but if you are not careful you may not be able to get at them, as in Figure 180.

Fig. 180

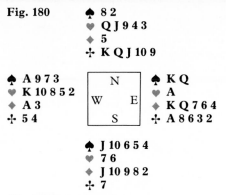

```
              ♠ 8 2
              ♥ Q J 9 4 3
              ♦ 5
              ♣ K Q J 10 9

♠ A 9 7 3         N         ♠ K Q
♥ K 10 8 5 2               ♥ A
♦ A 3        W      E      ♦ K Q 7 6 4
♣ 5 4             S        ♣ A 8 6 3 2

              ♠ J 10 6 5 4
              ♥ 7 6
              ♦ J 10 9 8 2
              ♣ 7
```

The bidding proceeds:

Fig. 181

West	*East*
Pass	1♦
1♥	2♣
2NT	3NT
Pass	

At his second turn East bids his clubs. Now West bids Two No-Trumps which like Two No-Trumps over an opening bid shows 11-12 points. East has ample strength to raise this to Three No-Trumps.

North leads the king of clubs. Before he plays from dummy West stops to plan. As always, the first thing he does is to count his tricks. You will find that counting the tricks is time and again the key to the correct play, either as declarer or as defender. On this hand West sees that he has three in spades (the ace, king and queen), two in hearts, three in diamonds and one in clubs. That is nine, sufficient for his contract. The only fly in the ointment is the *blockage* in the major suits. The tricks in these suits cannot be cashed without the aid of a side entry.

So West wins the club lead with the ace, and next cashes dummy's king, queen of spades and ace of hearts. Now that he has unblocked these suits he can come back to his hand with the ace of diamonds, cash his ace of spades and king of hearts, and return to dummy with a diamond to take his eighth and ninth tricks with the king and queen.

This hand is quite straightforward once you see the point. But if West had lazily ducked the opening lead (often the correct play in No-Trumps) North could have beaten the contract with an inspired switch to a diamond—this would remove West's entry before he had unblocked dummy's major suit winners.

Ducking and Holding-up

On the previous hand West had to win the first lead. But look at the deal in Figure 182.

Fig. 182

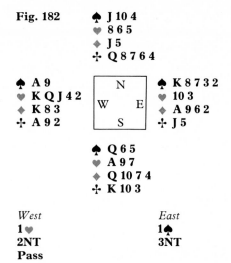

```
              ♠ J 10 4
              ♥ 8 6 5
              ♦ J 5
              ♣ Q 8 7 6 4

♠ A 9             N         ♠ K 8 7 3 2
♥ K Q J 4 2               ♥ 10 3
♦ K 8 3      W      E      ♦ A 9 6 2
♣ A 9 2           S        ♣ J 5

              ♠ Q 6 5
              ♥ A 9 7
              ♦ Q 10 7 4
              ♣ K 10 3
```

West	*East*
1♥	1♠
2NT	3NT
Pass	

West has the strength to open One No-Trump, but with his good five-card major suit opens One Heart. East shows his five-card spade suit, and West rebids Two No-Trumps, showing 17-18 points. East has just enough to give him Three No-Trumps.

North leads the six of clubs. Against a No-Trump contract it is generally best to lead the fourth highest of your longest suit. West sees that he has five tricks in top cards, and will have four more in hearts as soon as he has dislodged the ace. He puts on the jack of clubs from dummy in case North has led away from the king and queen (North would have made the same lead had his clubs been K Q 8 6 4), but South covers with the king. Now comes the critical play: West must *duck* South's king. If he takes the king with the ace and plays hearts, South will take his ace and play ten and another club enabling the defence to win one heart trick and four club tricks before West can take his hearts.

When the king of clubs holds the trick South continues with the ten. This West also ducks. South plays a third club which West has to take, but now when South wins his ace of hearts he does not have another club, and so he has to let West win the next trick with a spade or a diamond to cash his nine tricks.

Defensive Hold-ups. The hold-up technique works in exactly the same way for the defence. Figure 183 gives an example.

49

Fig. 183

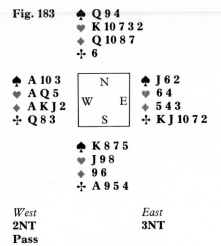

♠ Q 9 4
♥ K 10 7 3 2
♦ Q 10 8 7
♣ 6

♠ A 10 3   ♠ J 6 2
♥ A Q 5   ♥ 6 4
♦ A K J 2   ♦ 5 4 3
♣ Q 8 3   ♣ K J 10 7 2

♠ K 8 7 5
♥ J 9 8
♦ 9 6
♣ A 9 5 4

West	*East*
2NT	3NT
Pass	

North leads the three of hearts to the jack and queen. West sees that he will have nine tricks if he can score four club tricks. So at trick two he leads the queen of clubs. South does not take this trick as he can see the dummy has no entry apart from the club suit. At trick three West continues with a second club and North throws a spade. South can now work out that West has one more club, so he ducks again, thus holding the declarer to two club tricks and so defeating the contract.

Ducking to Preserve Entries. We saw in Chapter Two an example of ducking to produce an entry. That was in the layout repeated in Figure 184.

Fig. 184   Q 10 9

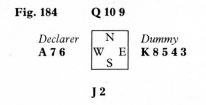

Declarer   N   *Dummy*
A 7 6   W   E   K 8 5 4 3
         S

J 2

To score four tricks in this suit at No-Trumps the declarer ducked the first round of the suit. There are many variations.

Fig. 185   K 9 6

Declarer   N   *Dummy*
5 4   W   E   A Q 8 7 3
         S

J 10 2

50   The first round in Figure 185 is ducked,

and the declarer then leads up towards the East hand for a second round finesse.

Fig. 186   J 3

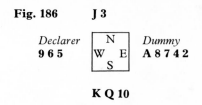

Declarer   N   *Dummy*
9 6 5   W   E   A 8 7 4 2
         S

K Q 10

The declarer in Figure 186 must duck twice, so that after he has lost two tricks the ace still remains in the East hand.

Sometimes the play of a suit is affected by the number of tricks required in it, as in Figure 187.

Fig. 187

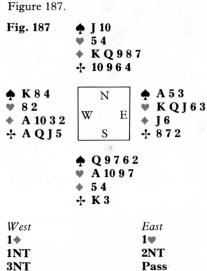

♠ J 10
♥ 5 4
♦ K Q 9 8 7
♣ 10 9 6 4

♠ K 8 4   ♠ A 5 3
♥ 8 2   ♥ K Q J 6 3
♦ A 10 3 2   ♦ J 6
♣ A Q J 5   ♣ 8 7 2

♠ Q 9 7 6 2
♥ A 10 9 7
♦ 5 4
♣ K 3

West	*East*
1♦	1♥
1NT	2NT
3NT	Pass

After West's rebid of One No-Trump East is good enough to suggest the possibility of game while not having quite enough to bid it himself. West has a good One No-Trump rebid, so goes to Three No-Trumps over East's invitation.

North's lead is something of a problem. While diamonds are his best suit they were the first suit bid by declarer; it is not on the whole a good idea to lead up to a suit bid on your right. So North leads the four of clubs to the two, king and ace.

After this friendly attack, West can count six tricks: two spades, one diamond and three clubs. If he tries to develop three more by leading a heart to dummy's king, all will be well if South wins. The declarer will subsequently concede a trick to South's ten, and re-enter dummy with the ace of spades to cash the fifth heart. But if South ducks the first heart, dummy's lack of entries will prevent the declarer from winning more than two heart tricks in all. The solution is for West to lead a heart at trick two and duck in dummy. South has to win, and whatever he does West can play his second heart and put on an honour, subsequently making three heart tricks for his contract. If you can understand this point immediately, you can probably afford to throw this book away.

Keeping out the Danger Hand
On many hands the declarer has to knock out more than one stopper. The theme of the hand in Figure 188 recurs frequently.

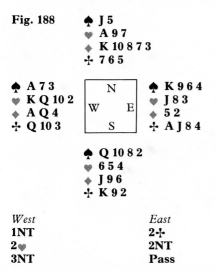

Fig. 188

	♠ J 5	
	♥ A 9 7	
	♦ K 10 8 7 3	
	♣ 7 6 5	

♠ A 7 3		♠ K 9 6 4
♥ K Q 10 2	N	♥ J 8 3
♦ A Q 4	W E	♦ 5 2
♣ Q 10 3	S	♣ A J 8 4

	♠ Q 10 8 2	
	♥ 6 5 4	
	♦ J 9 6	
	♣ K 9 2	

West	*East*
1NT	2♣
2♥	2NT
3NT	Pass

North leads the seven of diamonds to two, jack and queen. West has five tricks on top—two in spades, two in diamonds and one in clubs. He can develop three more in either hearts or clubs. The question is, which should he play on first?

Since it won't matter which suit he plays if the club finesse is right, he should assume that the club finesse is wrong. It appears from the lead that North holds the long suit in diamonds. It only remains for West to observe that in the club suit it is possible to keep North out of the lead, whereas in the heart suit there is nothing West can do if North has the ace.

At trick two then West leads hearts. North wins and attacks diamonds. West ducks the second round of diamonds, takes his ace on the third round. Now when he loses the club finesse to South, South has no more diamonds.

See what would happen if West had mistakenly played clubs first. South would have won and returned a diamond. Now

North clears the diamonds and still has the ace of hearts as an entry to his two winning diamonds.

The Play in Suit Contracts
If you decide to play in a suit contract rather than in No-Trumps, it is presumably because you think the trump element is going to be an advantage to you. But the defence will also have some trumps, and one of the most important decisions in the play of suit contracts is whether or when to *draw* their trumps.

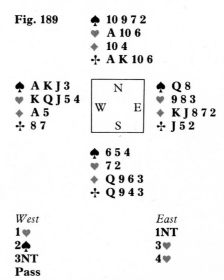

Fig. 189

	♠ 10 9 7 2	
	♥ A 10 6	
	♦ 10 4	
	♣ A K 10 6	

♠ A K J 3		♠ Q 8
♥ K Q J 5 4	N	♥ 9 8 3
♦ A 5	W E	♦ K J 8 7 2
♣ 8 7	S	♣ J 5 2

	♠ 6 5 4	
	♥ 7 2	
	♦ Q 9 6 3	
	♣ Q 9 4 3	

West	*East*
1♥	1NT
2♠	3♥
3NT	4♥
Pass	

In Figure 189 over East's One No-Trump response West *reverses* into Two Spades; the bid shows 17+ points with at least four spades, and longer hearts (with equal length in spades and hearts West would open One Spade). East has a minimum hand, so all he can do is prefer to Three Hearts. Within the limits of having at least four spades and at least five hearts West has a balanced hand; so he bids Three No-Trumps. But East rightly goes back to Four Hearts—his three-card support allied with a ruffing possibility in spades makes his hand more appropriate for the suit contract.

North leads ace, king and another club which West ruffs. On this hand the function of the trumps is simply to stop the run of the enemy's long suit. They are not needed for ruffing losers, so at trick four West leads a high heart from his hand. When North eventually wins with his ace of hearts, whatever he plays West will win and draw the remaining trumps before cashing his six winners in spades and diamonds.

On other hands it is wrong to draw trumps because dummy's trumps may be needed for ruffing the declarer's losers. Usually the symptom to look for is a shortage in dummy opposite an empty suit in the declarer's hand. We saw an example of that in Chapter Two. But sometimes it is not so obvious, as in Figure 190.

Fig. 190

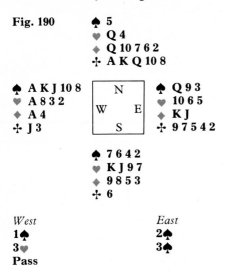

♠ 5
♥ Q 4
♦ Q 10 7 6 2
♣ A K Q 10 8

♠ A K J 10 8　　♠ Q 9 3
♥ A 8 3 2　　　　♥ 10 6 5
♦ A 4　　　　　　♦ K J
♣ J 3　　　　　　♣ 9 7 5 4 2

♠ 7 6 4 2
♥ K J 9 7
♦ 9 8 5 3
♣ 6

West	East
1♠	2♠
3♥	3♠
Pass	

West is worth an effort for game over Two Spades, so he makes a trial bid of Three Hearts. East has a minimum hand and a poor heart holding so he hastily signs off in Three Spades (incidentally, 'hastily' above is intended to be humorous; it is against the rules ever to give your partner an indication of your hand by any sort of intonation or mannerism).

North leads out three top clubs; on the second and third rounds South throws two diamonds. West ruffs the third club and takes stock. He knows he cannot establish a club trick for a heart discard, and at that point many players would think that their only chance of making the contract would be to find the outstanding hearts divided three and three. Then the declarer could win five trumps in his hand, ace and king of diamonds, ace of hearts and the thirteenth heart.

What is not so easy to spot is that the dummy has a ruffing value—it can ruff the fourth heart. All the declarer has to do is to lead ace and another heart at tricks four and five, and then another heart when he regains the lead, finally ruffing his fourth heart with one of dummy's high trumps. (A refinement is to cash the ace and king of diamonds first). Note that North could have defeated the contract had he switched to a trump after the second club; now each time South gets in on hearts he can play another trump, thus drawing all of dummy's in time to stop the declarer ruffing his fourth heart.

Chapter Ten

Defending

The difference between playing the dummy and defending is the partnership element. The declarer is not obliged to play his cards in a manner helpful to his partner. But the defenders must co-operate with one another if they are to put up an intelligent resistance.

The Opening Lead
The most critical play of a hand is often the opening lead. If you are lucky you may hold an *honour sequence*, that is a group of touching honours. Then it is usually correct to lead the top of the sequence.

Below are some examples:

Holding	Lead
K Q J	K
Q J 10	Q
Q J 9	Q
J 10 9	J
10 9 8	10
A K Q	K
A K J	K

You may notice an exception to the rule of 'top of a sequence' and that is from AK. The normal lead for this holding is the king, so the king lead is ambiguous, in that it can be either for K Q or A K.

Against No-Trump contracts, and sometimes against suits, it may be correct to lead from an *interior sequence*. This is an honour combination with a gap in it, and the correct lead is the top of the sequential part:

Holding	Lead
K J 10	**J**
K 10 9	**10**
A J 10	**J**
A 10 9	**10**
Q 10 9	**10**

Normally you are not so lucky as to have one of these holdings, and you may have to lead from a more ragged suit. If the suit is headed by an honour, it is usual to lead the *fourth best*.

Holding	Lead
Q 10 8 3	**3**
Q 10 8 3 2	**3**

Sometimes you may decide to lead from a holding which contains only small cards. There is a lot of dispute about what is the best card to lead from these combinations. However you won't go far wrong if you lead the top from a doubleton and either a middle card or fourth best from other holdings.

Play by Third Hand
There is an old rule-of-thumb which goes 'third player play high'. Like most rules of thumb there are lots of exceptions, but first of all let's see lay-outs where it is correct. In each case below West is the leader, and the card led is underlined.

Fig. 191   8 6 3

Q 9 4 <u>2</u>   [N W E S]   K <del>10</del> 7

A J 5

Players in the East seat in Figure 191 have a tendency not to play their king in this position. They put on the ten with some woolly notion of saving their king for later. But as you can see, the effect of that play is to let the declarer (South) score the jack. By playing the king East restricts the declarer to one trick in the suit.

Fig. 192   9 6 2

A 10 8 <u>3</u>   [N W E S]   K J 4

Q 7 5

Again in Figure 192 the message is the same: East must play the king to prevent the declarer making a trick in the suit.

Fig. 193   6 5 2

Q 8 7 <u>4</u>   [N W E S]   J 9 3

A K 10

If East in Figure 193 plays the jack the declarer can only make the ace and king.

Third player high also applies on some honour card leads, as in Figure 194.

Fig. 194   9 7 3

K J 10 8   [N W E S]   A 5 2

Q 6 4

If West has led from just J 10 8 x the declarer will always have two tricks with his holding of king-queen behind the ace. So East caters for West having led from an interior sequence, and puts on the ace.

Fig. 195   9 6 3

Q J 10 7 5   [N W E S]   A 8 4 2

K

If East ducks in Figure 195 the declarer will make his singleton king.
The Play from Sequences. Sometimes the third player will have a sequence in the suit led. The convention is to play the *lowest* card from the sequence. This helps to inform his partner of the lay-out of the suit.   53

Fig. 196

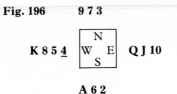

Fig. 196   9 7 3

K 8 5 **4**   [N W E S]   Q J 10

A 6 2

When the declarer wins East's 10 with the ace in Figure 196, West can work out that East must also have the queen and jack. But if East abandoned the convention and played say the queen, West would be entitled to assume the declarer held the jack. East's play of the queen *denies* holding the jack.

The rule of Eleven. One of the most useful gadgets for the defence is the rule of eleven. It arises from the convention of leading fourth best from holdings containing honours. It works like this: you subtract from eleven the number of the spot card led by your partner, and the answer gives you the number of cards held by the other three hands which are higher than the card partner has led. Some examples may help to make this less confusing:

i) Your partner leads the two of spades. Two from eleven leaves nine, so there must be nine cards held by the other three hands which are higher than the two. You can see that that must be so, because a) your partner can only have four cards in the suit—his fourth highest is the two b) there are twelve cards in the pack higher than the two and your partner is known to have three of them.

ii) Look at Figure 197.

Fig. 197   J 8 3

K 9 7 **6** 5   [N W E S]   Q 10 4

A 2

Your partner leads the six, the declarer (South) plays low from dummy, you play the ten and the declarer takes the ace. (Note that in this case you don't put on your highest card. You can see that with the jack on your right the ten will have the same effect as the queen—you have *finessed* against dummy's jack). Later in the hand you get in. Are you afraid to lead your queen lest the declarer have the king? You shouldn't be, if you understand the rule of

eleven. The short cut is to subtract six from eleven, leaving five. Hence five is the number of cards held between the dummy, you and the declarer which are higher than the six. Dummy and you have four between you, leaving one for the declarer which you have already seen. So you know that your partner must have the king.

Signalling

Groucho Marx used to tell his partners to nod their head and smile if they liked his lead. That of course is cheating. But the defence can communicate fairly, by means of card signals. The general idea is that if you throw a high card of a suit, you want your partner to lead or continue that suit; a low card has the opposite meaning.

Fig. 198   ♠ K 9 5 3
             ♥ 4
             ♦ J 3
             ♣ A K Q J 8 2

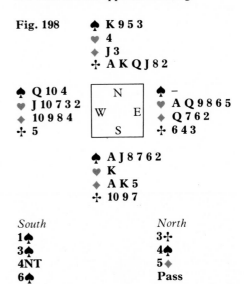

♠ Q 10 4   ♠ —
♥ J 10 7 3 2   ♥ A Q 9 8 6 5
♦ 10 9 8 4   ♦ Q 7 6 2
♣ 5   ♣ 6 4 3

             ♠ A J 8 7 6 2
             ♥ K
             ♦ A K 5
             ♣ 10 9 7

South	*North*
1♠	3♣
3♠	4♠
4NT	5♦
6♠	Pass

North in Figure 198 is worth a forcing take-out with his good spade fit and powerful club suit. South marks time with Three Spades, and North with nothing more to say raises to Four Spades. Now South bids Four No-Trumps. That is the **Blackwood** convention, and it asks his partner how many aces he has. The replies are Five Clubs for no aces, Five Diamonds for One, and so on up to Five No-Trumps for four. Rather like the point-count it is easy to understand and as a result is grossly mis-used. However South has an appropriate hand in this case, as he has first or second round control of the red suits.

The Five Diamond reply gives one ace, so South settles for Six Spades knowing that one ace is missing. West leads the ten of diamonds to jack, queen and ace. Note that South wins with the ace, not with the king, so as to produce confusion in the defence's minds as to who has the king. South now continues with the ace of spades and switches to clubs when he sees the bad trump break. He hopes that West will have to follow to three rounds of clubs so that he can discard his king of hearts before West can ruff in.

But West ruffs the second club. What should he play now? From his point of view East might have either the king of diamonds or the ace of hearts—the first round of diamonds was certainly consistent with East having the king-queen initially. The key to the whole hand is East's play on the first round of spades. He throws his *nine* of hearts, a signal indicating his strength in that suit. Thus he helps West to find the correct switch.

Chapter Eleven
Defensive Bidding

Up to this point we have only considered uncontested auctions. But often the opponents have opened the bidding before you have had a chance to say anything. Then you must consider whether your hand is good enough to intervene.

Overcall in a Suit

Fig. 199

Fig. 200

If you were the dealer on the two hands in Figures 199 and 200, you would pass on the first and open One Club on the second. Yet

if the bidding were opened on your right with One Club, it would be correct to overcall with One Spade on Figure 199, but quite wrong to do so on Figure 200. That brings us to an important point—an essential feature of an overcall is that it must have a reasonable suit.

The normal minimum strength of the suit is about K 10 x x x. The reason that I lay much more emphasis on suit strength is that when you intervene over an opening bid you are taking a risk in that your opponents may be able to double you. If you overcall One Spade on the hand in Figure 200 and that is doubled, your smattering of points is not going to help you make tricks unless your partner has a good hand. But in Figure 199 your hand is already worth three to four tricks in spades even if your partner has very little.

Overcalls are rather more affected by vulnerability than are opening bids. When you are vulnerable it is riskier to intervene because the penalties are more if you are

Fig. 201

Fig. 202

Fig. 205

Fig. 203

Fig. 206

doubled and go down. Some examples are given in Figures 201 to 203.

Figure 201 is worth an overcall of One Spade not vulnerable. If you were vulnerable it would be wiser to pass as your spades are too ragged. Figure 202 is a sound overcall of One Heart, as the good suit compensates for the lack of high card strength. But the hand is not strong enough for an overcall at the Two level, so you would pass an opening bid of One Spade.

Figure 203, though it has more in high cards than either Figures 201 or 202, does not merit an overcall of any opening bid. Since an overcall is normally based on a good suit your partner will trustingly lead that suit if the opponents eventually play the contract. With Figure 203 you certainly don't want to divert your partner from his natural lead, so it is best not to get involved in the auction.

Two level overcalls have to be distinctly stronger than those at the One level. You

usually need a six-card suit, and getting on for opening strength in high cards, as in Figures 204 to 206.

Figure 204 is adequate for a non-vulnerable overcall of Two Hearts over One Spade, but you wouldn't be surprised if you gave a penalty. It is too weak to overcall vulnerable. Figure 205 is a sound Two Heart bid at any vulnerability. Note the difference that the intermediate cards in the heart suit make. In Figure 204 you cannot guarantee to make more than one heart trick, in Figure 205 you have a certain four heart tricks. Figure 206 is about a minimum for an overcall based on a five-card suit. Change the ten of diamonds into the two, and the hand would be too weak.

The upper limit of strength for a simple overcall (i.e. one made at the minimum level) is about 15 points. Stronger hands have to be treated differently (see below).

The Jump Overcall

A jump overcall is an overcall which jumps one level of bidding. If your right hand opponent opens One Club and you bid a suit at the Two level, that is a jump overcall. Some years ago a jump overcall was used to show a very strong hand. However with the passage of time there has been an erosion of the values required, till nowadays the most common type is the *intermediate jump overcall*. This shows a hand which is worth a sound opening with a good six-card suit.

Fig. 204

Fig. 207

Fig. 208

Fig. 209

opening bid. So the responder has a rather better idea of what to expect.

Raises. Three-card support is quite adequate to raise an overcall. After all, your partner will practically always have at least a five card suit.

Fig. 210

Your left-hand opponent (LHO) opens One Club, your partner overcalls One Heart, your right hand opponent (RHO) passes. With the hand in Figure 210 you raise to Two Hearts. Note that you don't bid One Spade. That investigatory bid is not necessary in this sequence, as you already know you have a good heart fit.

You need a little more strength to give a double raise than you do opposite an opening bid, as your partner may have less than opening strength. Consider Figures 211 and 212.

Fig. 211

Fig. 212

While Figure 207 is a sound opening bid of One Spade, it is only worth a simple overcall because of the weakness of the spade suit. Figure 208 though a fairly minimum opening bid, is worth a jump overcall of Two Spades. Figure 209 is about the least you need for a jump to the Three level over a major suit opening.

Another style of jump overcall that is being played more is the **weak jump overcall**. This style of overcall again shows a six-card suit, though not necessarily so strong as that required for an intermediate jump. The general strength however is in the 7–10 HCP range, rather less than an opening bid. This style is not suited to inexperienced players, and I recommend that you use the 'intermediate jump' method.

Responding to an Overcall

The first thing to note is that an overcall has a narrower range of strength than an

Figure 211 would be worth Three Spades over an opening One Spade, but it is only worth Two Spades after an overcall of One Spade. Figure 212 merits a raise to Three Spades opposite a One Spade overcall. Note that the double raise can be made with three card support.

Responses in No-Trumps. No-Trump responses are made on much the same types of hand as those that reply in No-Trumps to opening bids. However the strength needs to be a little greater, to allow for the overcaller's possible deficiency in high cards. And the responder needs a good stopper, preferably two stoppers, in the opponents' suit.

Fig. 213

Fig. 214

In Figure 213 respond One No-Trump after LHO opens One Heart and your partner overcalls One Spade. Figure 214 is about minimum for a Two No-Trump bid after the same start to the auction.
Response in a New Suit. A simple change of suit is played as not forcing. Note the difference from the change of suit over an

Fig. 215

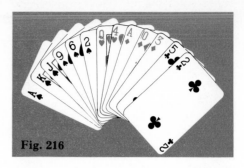
Fig. 216

opening bid. If the responder wants to force the opener to bid again he must jump in a new suit, and even that is only a one round force, not a game force.

In Figure 215 respond One Spade after partner has made a One level overcall. With the hand in Figure 216 you have enough to bid Two Spades.

Overcall in No-Trumps
When you have a balanced hand of 16-18 points you may be able to overcall with One No-Trump.

Fig. 217

Fig. 218

With the hands in Figures 217 and 218 overcall One Heart with One No-Trump. The partner of the overcaller responds in much the same way as to an opening of One No-Trump.

The Take-out Double
One of the most useful weapons available to the defending side is the ***take-out*** or

informatory double. Consider Figure 219, which shows how useful this weapon can be when properly used.

Fig. 219

Your right-hand opponent opens One Heart. It is not satisfactory to overcall with either Two Clubs or One Spade and you might think that therefore you would have to pass. But by agreement a Double of a One level opening bid in a suit is a *take-out double*. That is, the doubler

Fig. 220

Fig. 221

Fig. 222

is asking his partner to bid. Ideally the doubler should have support for the other three suits as in Figure 219. His strength should be at least equal to an opening bid, though he may be very much stronger. On all the hands in Figures 220 to 222 the correct bid when One Diamond is opened on your right is Double.

Figure 220 is a minimum, and the doubler will leave subsequent bidding to his partner. With the hand in Figure 221 the doubler may be prepared to push on should his partner make a game try, and in Figure 222 the double is extremely strong and will issue a game invitation on the next round.

A take-out double may also be the best move on less suitable shapes, as in Figures 223 and 224.

Fig. 223

Fig. 224

In Figure 223 you double One Diamond and then bid Two Spades if your partner responds Two Clubs. He will realise you must be better than a minimum for your double – otherwise you would have passed Two Clubs. In Figure 224 you double any opening bid, and then rebid Two No-Trumps to show you have a balanced 20-22 points.

Responding to a Take-out Double. The responder replies as though his partner had a hand like Figure 220 above. With less than about 9 or 10 points he simply bids his best suit. With a five-card suit and 10 points or so he can make a jump response, which is not forcing. He can reply in No-Trumps if he has a balanced hand with stoppers in the oponent's suit. Or he can make the strongest possible bid, that of making a **cue-bid** in the opponent's suit (see below).

On each of the hands in Figures 225 to 230 the auction starts LHO One Diamond, your partner Double, RHO pass.
In Figure 225 you bid One Spade. In Figure 226 you have enough to bid Two

Fig. 229

Fig. 225

Fig. 230

Fig. 226

Spades. Now if your partner is better than a minimum he can bid on and you may reach game. In Figure 227 you respond One No-Trump. With the hand in Figure 228 you pass One Diamond doubled; the only type of hand on which you should ever pass the double is one where you have long and solid trumps. Your partner should lead a diamond if One Diamond doubled becomes the final contract.

Figure 229 is worth a Four Spade bid – even if your partner has a minimum double there will be a play for it. Figure 230 involves a new notion. Obviously if your partner has an opening bid you have enough strength between you to make a game. But if you take a stab at say Four Hearts you may find that your partner has three hearts and four spades, and Four Spades may be a better contract.

Clearly you would like to make a forcing bid, simply asking your partner to bid his best suit. Luckily there is an entirely logical forcing bid available: **Two Diamonds**. This bid of the opponent's suit is called a **cue-bid**, and has a variety of uses. In this instance your partner can work out that you can't want to play in a contract of Two Diamonds. If that were the case you would pass One Diamond Doubled. So the cue-bid is used as a general force; whichever major suit the doubler bids in reply to the cue bid, the responder will raise to game.

Fig. 227

Fig. 228

Appendix
How to Improve

This book is necessarily a very brief survey of the sorts of things you need to know about how to play bridge. While the main emphasis has been on rubber bridge, any keen player should play *duplicate bridge* from time to time. In duplicate bridge the cards from the individual hands are not mixed together at the end of the play, but are kept in separate holders. In this way the same deal can be played by several different groups of people, and their results compared. This is a good way to learn, as you see what the possibilities are and can discuss with other players their approach to a particular hand. Most cities and towns have a duplicate bridge club, and these are usually willing to take on beginners.

Further Reading

There is an extensive literature on bridge. Below I give a list of books that are suitable for beginners, though there are many which are not included that other experts would recommend.

Bidding and Play

Bridge by Terence Reese (Penguin, Harmondsworth, 1970)
Contract Bridge Complete by Charles Goren (George Coffin, Mass., 1952)
How to Play a Good Game of Bridge by Terence Reese and Albert Dormer (Heinemann, London, 1969 and Pan Books, London, 1971)
The Complete Book of Bridge by Terence Reese and Albert Dormer (Faber & Faber, London, 1973)

Bidding

Bridge Bidding Made Easy by Edwin Kantar (Wilshire Book Co., Ca.)
Bridge Conventions by Edwin Kantar (Wilshire Book Co., Ca.)
Bridge : Modern Bidding by Victor Mollo (Faber & Faber, London, 1966)
The Acol System Today by Terence Reese and Albert Dormer (Edward Arnold, London, 1961)

Play

Card Play Technique by Victor Mollo and Nico Gardener (Faber & Faber, London, 1971)
Introduction to Declarer's Play by Edwin Kantar (Prentice-Hall, N.J., 1968)
Introduction to Defender's Play by Edwin Kantar (Prentice-Hall, N.J., 1968)
The Play of the Cards by Terence Reese and Albert Dormer (Penguin, Harmondsworth, 1971)
Reese on Play by Terence Reese (Edward Arnold, London, 1948)

General

Bid Boldly, Play Safe by Rixi Markus (Hawthorn Books, New York, 1968)
Tiger Bridge by Jeremy Flint and Freddie North (Hodder, London, 1970)
Story of an Accusation by Terence Reese (Heinemann, London, 1966)
Bridge for Tournament Players by Terence Reese and Albert Dormer (Hale & Co., Wis., 1968)

Index